**INTRODUCING
ISSUES WITH
OPPOSING
VIEWPOINTS**®

Student
Protests

Martin Gitlin, Book Editor

GREENHAVEN
PUBLISHING

Published in 2020 by Greenhaven Publishing, LLC
353 3rd Avenue, Suite 255, New York, NY 10010

Copyright © 2020 by Greenhaven Publishing, LLC

First Edition

Articles in Greenhaven Publishing anthologies are often edited for length to meet page requirements. In addition, original titles of these works are changed to clearly present the main thesis and to explicitly indicate the author's opinion. Every effort is made to ensure that Greenhaven Publishing accurately reflects the original intent of the authors. Every effort has been made to trace the owners of the copyrighted material.

Library of Congress Cataloging-in-Publication Data

Names: Gitlin, Marty, editor.
Title: Student protests / Martin Gitlin, editor
Description: First edition. | New York : Greenhaven Publishing, [2020] |
  Series: Introducing issues with opposing viewpoints | Audience: Grades
  7-12. | Includes bibliographical references and index.
Identifiers: LCCN 2018056917| ISBN 9781534505742 (library bound) | ISBN
  9781534505759 (pbk.)
Subjects: LCSH: Students—Political activity—United States—Juvenile
  literature. | Student movements—United States—Juvenile literature. |
  Youth movements—United States--Juvenile literature.
Classification: LCC LB3610 .S84 2020 | DDC 371.8/10973—dc23
LC record available at https://lccn.loc.gov/2018056917

Manufactured in the United States of America

Website: http://greenhavenpublishing.com

Contents

Chapter 1: How Should Schools Approach Student Protests?

Chapter 2: Are Student Protesters Tolerant of Other Perspectives?

Chapter 3: Is Violence Ever Justified?

Foreword

Indulging in a wide spectrum of ideas, beliefs, and perspectives is a critical cornerstone of democracy. After all, it is often debates over differences of opinion, such as whether to legalize abortion, how to treat prisoners, or when to enact the death penalty, that shape our society and drive it forward. Such diversity of thought is frequently regarded as the hallmark of a healthy and civilized culture. As the Reverend Clifford Schutjer of the First Congregational Church in Mansfield, Ohio, declared in a 2001 sermon, "Surrounding oneself with only like-minded people, restricting what we listen to or read only to what we find agreeable is irresponsible. Refusing to entertain doubts once we make up our minds is a subtle but deadly form of arrogance." With this advice in mind, Introducing Issues with Opposing Viewpoints books aim to open readers' minds to the critically divergent views that comprise our world's most important debates.

Introducing Issues with Opposing Viewpoints simplifies for students the enormous and often overwhelming mass of material now available via print and electronic media. Collected in every volume is an array of opinions that captures the essence of a particular controversy or topic. Introducing Issues with Opposing Viewpoints books embody the spirit of nineteenth-century journalist Charles A. Dana's axiom: "Fight for your opinions, but do not believe that they contain the whole truth, or the only truth." Absorbing such contrasting opinions teaches students to analyze the strength of an argument and compare it to its opposition. From this process readers can inform and strengthen their own opinions, or be exposed to new information that will change their minds. Introducing Issues with Opposing Viewpoints is a mosaic of different voices. The authors are statesmen, pundits, academics, journalists, corporations, and ordinary people who have felt compelled to share their experiences and ideas in a public forum. Their words have been collected from newspapers, journals, books, speeches, interviews, and the Internet, the fastest growing body of opinionated material in the world.

Introducing Issues with Opposing Viewpoints shares many of the well-known features of its critically acclaimed parent series, Opposing

Viewpoints. The articles allow readers to absorb and compare divergent perspectives. Active reading questions preface each viewpoint, requiring the student to approach the material thoughtfully and carefully. Photographs, charts, and graphs supplement each article. A thorough introduction provides readers with crucial background on an issue. An annotated bibliography points the reader toward articles, books, and websites that contain additional information on the topic. An appendix of organizations to contact contains a wide variety of charities, nonprofit organizations, political groups, and private enterprises that each hold a position on the issue at hand. Finally, a comprehensive index allows readers to locate content quickly and efficiently.

Introducing Issues with Opposing Viewpoints is also significantly different from Opposing Viewpoints. As the series title implies, its presentation will help introduce students to the concept of opposing viewpoints and learn to use this material to aid in critical writing and debate. The series' four-color, accessible format makes the books attractive and inviting to readers of all levels. In addition, each viewpoint has been carefully edited to maximize a reader's understanding of the content. Short but thorough viewpoints capture the essence of an argument. A substantial, thought-provoking essay question placed at the end of each viewpoint asks the student to further investigate the issues raised in the viewpoint, compare and contrast two authors' arguments, or consider how one might go about forming an opinion on the topic at hand. Each viewpoint contains sidebars that include at-a-glance information and handy statistics. A Facts About section located in the back of the book further supplies students with relevant facts and figures.

Following in the tradition of the Opposing Viewpoints series, Greenhaven Publishing continues to provide readers with invaluable exposure to the controversial issues that shape our world. As John Stuart Mill once wrote: "The only way in which a human being can make some approach to knowing the whole of a subject is by hearing what can be said about it by persons of every variety of opinion and studying all modes in which it can be looked at by every character of mind. No wise man ever acquired his wisdom in any mode but this." It is to this principle that Introducing Issues with Opposing Viewpoints books are dedicated.

Introduction

"No kid should be afraid to go to school, no kid should be afraid to walk outside, and no kid should have to worry about being shot. Now that's why I'm marching."
—*Marjory Stoneman Douglas High School student Alfonso Calderon*

Call them protests against protests. But many in the older generations, some of whom might have marched for civil rights and against the Vietnam War a half-century ago, have expressed outrage over the motivations and tactics of modern-day demonstrators.

They lodge several complaints. Among them is their view that students should focus on their studies and leave the problems of the world to lawmakers. Adults that rail against young people protesting in the streets claim that those on high school and college campuses are reacting emotionally rather than intellectually to events such as mass shootings and racism. They contend that kids should learn more about issues, then work within the system to create change.

Another grievance voiced by those protesting protests revolves around the silencing of those with distasteful worldviews. Many demonstrations in recent years, particularly on college campuses, have been inspired by the impending arrival of speakers spewing hateful rhetoric. Comparatively few people agree with their opinions, but many more have asserted that constitutional guarantees of freedom of speech must be recognized and preserved. They claim that students have no right to demand that speakers with whom they disagree, no matter how vile, be banned from their schools.

A third objection revolves around violent protest. Though most demonstrators remain peaceful, some belong to organizations that promote violence as a means of forcing change or simply allow their anger to overwhelm their sense of calm. Many feel that violence not only begets violence but is also a surefire way to lose potential public support.

While all three contentions boast some merit, each can be rightfully disputed. One can argue that school is all about learning—and not just in the classroom. If students have indeed gained enough knowledge about issues concerning their country and the world to form strong opinions and are inspired to protest, that speaks volumes about what they have absorbed both on and off their campuses. It can be rightfully stated that active learning experiences are more valuable than those that result from silent studies.

The belief that neither students nor anyone else have the right to attempt to ban speakers with white nationalist or other far-right views can be disputed in a historical context. After all, would it have not potentially saved the world from a war that cost fifty million lives had successful protests toppled the Nazi regime in Germany in the 1930s? There is a fine line between free speech and hate speech that can be interpreted as promoting violence against racial or sexual minorities. The US Constitution does not protect the voicing of such views. And do provocateurs who spew hate and intolerance own the right to do so in public? Those involved in student protests do not believe so.

But should they use violence to prevent violence? That is the thorniest issue of all. Protests often exploded into violence during the civil rights movement and Vietnam War era of the 1960s and 1970s. Most applicable to this subject were violent campus protests against the war. One such demonstration at Kent State University in Ohio resulted in the deaths of four students after the National Guard opened fire on protesters.

Violence in nearly all such cases is the product of frustration. African Americans involved in dozens of inner city insurrections, mostly from 1964 to 1968, had grown increasingly angry over the racism and discrimination that prevented them from achieving the same rights afforded white citizens for centuries. And young antiwar protesters had become more infuriated and frustrated over the continued killing of thousands of their generation in Vietnamese jungles halfway around the world. Their argument in favor of violent protest was that peaceful demonstrations had accomplished little.

Those who disagree with that contention would cite student groups such as the Freedom Riders of the early 1960s, who remained peaceful in the face of the most brutal violence of bigots during the civil rights era, called national attention to racism in the Jim Crow South, and helped force legislation such as the Voting Rights Act and Civil Rights Act. Students heeded the call for nonviolence while being beaten and arrested sitting at lunch counters for integration as disciples of Dr. Martin Luther King Jr. They raised the consciousness and morality of Americans and their government.

Perhaps the most pressing issue for modern students is gun violence. It is no wonder considering the seemingly unending number of mass shootings that have desecrated institutions of learning since the 1999 Columbine High School massacre. Students who believe they should feel safe in their schools have staged walkouts and other forms of protest. They cite the fact that such killings have occurred and indeed grown in frequency over the last two decades, and they hear nothing but "thoughts and prayers" coming from their nation's leaders. The same level of anger and frustration that inspired previous generations to protest, sometimes even violently, has taken hold of the current generation of students.

Students seek a better world for themselves and future generations. Coupled with the inalienable American right to protest, their desires and actions have caused controversy. But their activism is refreshing to many Americans who have decried the crass materialism and self-centered attitudes of many young people in previous decades. The diverse viewpoints in *Introducing Issues with Opposing Viewpoints: Student Protests* explore the many angles of this contentious issue.

Chapter 1

How Should Schools Approach Student Protests?

The shooting at Marjory Stoneman Douglas prompted high school students across the country to protest.

Viewpoint

1

Schools Were Tested on Walkout Wednesday

"Many students and organizers have been clear that they believe the walkout is and should be considered a political protest."

Cory Turner and Clare Lombardo

In the following excerpted viewpoint, Cory Turner and Clare Lombardo examine the reaction of various administrations to what was then the impending walkout of students to protest gun violence in schools. Many educators feared that the planned 17-minute student walkout would prove disruptive to the school-day structure. But others implicitly railed against any level of politicization of students. The authors also focus on reactions of other school officials representing various systems around the country. Turner is senior editor and Lombardo a news assistant at National Public Radio.

AS YOU READ, CONSIDER THE FOLLOWING QUESTIONS:
1. Did the Needville superintendent provide viable reasoning in banning students from protesting?
2. How was a 1969 Supreme Court case involving a student in Iowa made relevant in this article?
3. Which school system mentioned here was most open to a student walkout and why did it allow one?

Wednesday morning, at 10 o'clock, students at schools across the country will walk out of their classrooms. The plan is for them to leave school—or at least gather in the hallway—for 17 minutes. That's one minute for each of the victims in last month's school shooting in Parkland, Fla.

The walkout has galvanized teens nationwide and raised big questions for schools about how to handle protests.

The organizers, Women's March Youth EMPOWER, have made it clear: While this walkout is meant to honor the victims in Parkland, as well as anyone who's experienced gun violence, it is also a political call to action.

"It's about protesting Congress' inaction when it comes to gun violence," says Kaleab Jegol, a 17-year-old high school senior and protest coordinator from Ohio.

Organizers have posted their demands online, including an assault weapons ban and expanded background checks. Jegol knows, their protest isn't sitting well with some school leaders. In Needville, Texas, Superintendent Curtis Rhodes issued a stern warning to students and parents:

> The Needville ISD is very sensitive to violence in schools including the recent incident in Florida. Anytime an individual deliberately chooses to harm others, we are sensitive and compassionate to those impacted. There is a "movement" attempting to stage walkouts/disruptions of the school through social media and/or other media outlets
>
> Please be advised that the Needville ISD will not allow a student demonstration during school hours for any type of protest or awareness!! Should students choose to do so, they will be suspended from school for 3 days and face all the consequences that come along with an out of school suspension. Life is all about choices and every choice has a consequence whether it be positive or negative. We will discipline no matter if it is one, fifty, or five hundred students involved. All will be suspended for 3 days and parent notes will not alleviate the discipline.

A school is a place to learn and grow educationally, emotionally and morally. A disruption of the school will not be tolerated.

Respect yourself, your fellow students and the Needville Independent School District and please understand that we are here for an education and not a political protest.

Curtis Rhodes
Superintendent of Schools

Needville High School's Facebook page, where the letter was posted, has since been taken down. Rhodes did not respond to an interview request, but the district tells NPR that it stands by its suspension threat. This is why, Jegol says, students need to know their rights.

"If it's possible to work with [your school's] administration, then great," Jegol says. "But if consequences like suspension are being threatened, students still do have those First Amendment rights."

Turns out, this walkout is a fascinating walk—out onto a tight-rope, stretched between students' free speech rights and schools' legal obligations. And like any tightrope, this one's full of tension.

Students' Free Speech Rights

"It can hardly be argued that either students or teachers shed their constitutional rights to freedom of speech or expression at the school-house gate."

So wrote a 7–2 majority of the US Supreme Court in 1969, after hearing the case of Mary Beth Tinker. The Des Moines teenager had worn a black armband to school, in protest of the Vietnam War, and school leaders suspended her for it. The court sided with Tinker because, the justices reasoned, her protest did not "materially and substantially disrupt the work and discipline of the school."

A walkout, though, is no armband, and likely exceeds students' free speech protections.

"Is [the demonstration] going to be disruptive to the learning and educational mission of the school?" asks Esha Bhandari, a staff

Public school students have free speech rights on school campuses during school hours, but these rights are limited.

attorney with the American Civil Liberties Union. If so, Bhandari says, then schools are within their rights to intervene and even punish students.

Some schools have promised not to punish students who walk out. Others have said the walkout will be considered an unexcused absence and punished accordingly, usually gently. For schools like those in Needville, that have promised harsher punishment, Bhandari has a warning:

"Students shouldn't be punished any differently than any other unexplained or unexcused absence would be. I think that's the really critical distinction here."

It all comes down to pre-existing district policy. If the student code of conduct says skipping class should trigger a note home or detention, then school leaders can't start handing out three-day suspensions. If they do, it could be argued, they're punishing students for their political speech, not for their actions.

So what should schools do?

Schools' Options and Responsibilities

We'll be a little reductive here, but it's worth mapping out schools' basic options in response to the walkout. And you'll see, there are no basic options.

Instead of attempting to shut down the walkout before it starts with threats of harsh punishment, principals could head in the opposite direction, just letting students walk. But, that's complicated, too.

"Schools stand in what's known as loco parentis, so we don't simply release our students into the ether," says Francisco Negron, Chief Legal Officer at the National School Boards Association.

"In loco parentis" is a legal term, and it means schools are legally obligated to safeguard students. The irony is that this walkout is all about keeping students safe, but that's also why school leaders don't want to let them walk out. Negron recently sent guidance to districts to help them walk this tightrope.

Instead, many districts have said they'll allow the walkout—but only for students whose parents sign them out or sign a permission slip.

In an effort to keep students inside, some schools have talked about trying to turn the walkout into an assembly, to give protesters a safe forum. But Negron warns that even this can be tricky:

"When you open up a forum for protests to happen, then you open up the possibility that those parties that you don't allow in could claim that you're discriminating on the basis of viewpoint."

That's why, when administrators in Gwinnett County, Ga., announced that they could not condone a student walkout, they spelled out why: enforcing school rules for some protests but not others is grounds for a First Amendment violation.

Some schools have tried to protect themselves from such a charge of discrimination by arguing that the walkout or assembly they've sanctioned is an apolitical event meant to commemorate the victims in the Parkland shooting. The problem is, as we've said, many students and organizers have been clear that they believe the walkout is and should be considered a political protest.

Perhaps the best plan for schools is also the most complicated—and creative.

Administrators in Wallingford, Conn., have offered students there a variety of alternatives to the walkout, including time to write letters to their representatives or complete homework in study hall.

Thirty minutes north, in Hartford, Conn., "Staff, administration, and students will be walking out, down to our football field, and we will stand there in silence for 17 minutes," says Gage Salicki, who teaches social studies at Bulkeley High School.

So the walkout will happen at Bulkeley, but that's only half the story.

"In preparation for this walkout, we asked that students design something related to civic action," Salicki says.

In fact, Salicki helped build a multi-day lesson plan around the walkout—one he began teaching last week. His class watched cell phone footage taken by students during the shooting at Marjory Stoneman Douglas High School and explored all sides of America's raging gun debate.

"We wanted to make sure that students, if delving into some heavy legal territory related to Second Amendment rights, would have equal access to the pros and cons of the issue," Salicki says.

The school's approach wasn't to shy away from politics but to give students a range of resources and encourage them to think critically about the facts. Students were then asked to do one of a few things: make a poster to carry during the walkout, write a letter to a person in power or write a song or poem about what they've learned.

Salicki hopes they've turned this tension-filled moment into a teachable moment.

The First Amendment Does Not Give Public High School Students a Right to Walk Out

"Punishing students for a brief but important moment of political activism may be sending the wrong message about freedom of speech in a democratic society."

Clay Calvert

In the following viewpoint Clay Calvert argues that, although public schools have the legal right to punish students for participating in a walkout protest, he believes that they would be better served by embracing the event as a way to teach kids about civic responsibility and the impact of dissent on US history. The author cites the lunch counter sit-ins of the early 1960s in which students and others peacefully forced integration in the South. Calvert is director of the Marion B. Brechner First Amendment Project.

"What the National School Walkout Says About Schools and Free Speech," by Clay Calvert, The Conversation, March 14, 2018. https://theconversation.com/what-the-national-school-walkout-says-about-schools-and-free-speech-93327. Licensed under CC BY-ND 4.0.

1. Is it unfair that the First Amendment protects the freedom of speech for public school students and not private school students?
2. Does the author maintain objectivity throughout?
3. Should schools have punished students for their walkout or used the event as a lesson in the importance of political protest in American history?

Thousands of high school students across the nation left their classes March 14 precisely at 10 a.m. for 17 minutes.

The walkout served two purposes: to honor the 17 people —including 14 students—killed exactly one month ago at Marjory Stoneman Douglas High School in Parkland, Florida, and to call for stronger gun control laws.

Organized by a Women's March unit called Youth Empower and promoted on Twitter with the hashtags #Enough and #NationalSchoolWalkout, students throughout the country took to the streets and gathered at various places to call attention to the problem of gun violence in schools and in their communities.

Some schools are threatening to punish these young activists. But others are trying to work with them. As one article put it, "The response from school districts has been mixed, with some threatening to suspend students and others promising to incorporate the walkout into a civics lesson."

Enter the First Amendment

From my standpoint as director of the Marion B. Brechner First Amendment Project at the University of Florida, all of this raises important questions about the scope of First Amendment speech rights for high school students. Are the students who exit their classes immune from punishment?

A starting point for answering this question is to understand that the First Amendment only protects against government censorship,

Was Walkout Wednesday also a teaching opportunity for educators?

not censorship by private entities. Thus, only public school students have First Amendment speech rights. Private school students do not.

California is an exception to this rule. It has a statute known as the Leonard Law that extends First Amendment speech rights to students at private nonreligious high schools. No other state has such a statute.

From Black Armbands to Student Walkouts

The second point is that the US Supreme Court recognized in 1969 in a case called *Tinker v. Des Moines Independent Community School District* that public high school students do have First Amendment speech rights while on campus. Those rights are limited, however. Specifically, the right of free speech ends when there are facts that might reasonably lead "school authorities to forecast substantial disruption of or material interference with school activities."

In *Tinker*, the Supreme Court ruled in favor of several students who wore black armbands to their schools to protest the war in Vietnam and to support a truce over the winter holidays. There was simply no evidence that the passive expression of a political viewpoint on a sleeve might substantially and materially disrupt educational activities.

Like *Tinker*, the student walkouts today are a form of political expression and, in particular, dissenting political expression because the students object to current gun laws. Such speech lies at the heart of the First Amendment.

As Justice Anthony Kennedy wrote for the court in a nonstudent speech case in 2010, "Speech is an essential mechanism of democracy, for it is the means to hold officials accountable to the people." He added that "political speech must prevail against laws that would suppress it, whether by design or inadvertence." With today's walkouts, students want to hold lawmakers accountable for what they view as lax gun control laws.

Not Immune from Punishment

School officials who punish students for walking out of class today have the right to do so as long as they are enforcing regular attendance policies in a consistent manner. They could also argue that leaving class for 17 minutes amounts to a substantial and material disruption of educational activities, per the rule from *Tinker*.

On the other hand, missing 17 minutes out of a school day and, in turn, an entire school year seems neither substantially nor materially disruptive. Punishing students for a brief but important moment of political activism may be sending the wrong message about freedom of speech in a democratic society.

Many universities have said they will not hold it against applicants who are punished due to today's walkout. As Richard H. Shaw, dean of undergraduate admission and financial aid at Stanford University, stated, "Given the nature of this national tragedy and the true and heartfelt response of students in expressing their perspectives and expectations, the University will not consider the choice of students to participate in protests as a factor in the review of present or future candidates."

The Price of Civil Disobedience

So the choice to walk out and face possible punishment ultimately is left to the students. Sometimes that choice may be worth it. As Frank LoMonte, director of the Brechner Center for Freedom of Information at the University of Florida recently put it:

> *The effectiveness of "civil disobedience" has always depended on a willingness to throw yourself in the way, whether that is sitting-in at a lunch counter or occupying the university president's office. But that also means accepting that disciplinary or even legal consequences may result.*

The bottom line is that the First Amendment does not give public high school students a right to walk out of classes. It does, however, give administrators a critical justification for shielding them from punishment and to take advantage of a teachable moment about the importance of political protest in the United States.

EVALUATING THE AUTHOR'S ARGUMENTS:

How does the viewpoint author use law, history, and communication in reporting on Walkout Wednesday to convey his perspective? Is this a more effective method than straight reporting or straight opinion?

Protests Are Opportunities to Teach Civil Disobedience

"At a time when civic participation is soured by public distrust in the political process, the walkouts present a chance for students to model responsible citizenship."

Abena Hutchful

In the following viewpoint Abena Hutchful argues for the rights of students to participate in Walkout Wednesday and contends that teachers should encourage their students to do so. The author believes it is not only their First Amendment right to free speech but a valuable civics lesson as well for students to understand that they can play a role in creating political change in their country while standing up for what they believe. Hutchful is a human rights lawyer who coordinates the Youth Free Expression Program for the National Coalition Against Censorship.

AS YOU READ, CONSIDER THE FOLLOWING QUESTIONS:

1. Does the author give strong reasoning in asserting that teachers should encourage students to stage a walkout?
2. What arguments could you raise against the view that teachers should urge students to protest?
3. How do this author and the author of the previous article differ in regard to rights provided students by the First Amendment?

"Teachers, Tell Your Students to Walk Out on Wednesday," by Abena Hutchful, March 13, 2018. Reprinted by permission.

Wednesday is walkout day. The school protest marches planned are the first in a series of student-led actions, part of a massive student-planned response to the mass shooting at Florida's Marjory Stoneman Douglas High School. Seventeen people, 14 of them students, were killed in that massacre last month. Over half of the 97 mass public shootings to occur in the United States over the past 30 years have happened in schools or workplaces. The students of America have had enough.

The walkouts present an opportunity for students to express their frustration in a way that inspires actual change. At a time when civic participation is soured by public distrust in the political process, the walkouts present a chance for students to model responsible citizenship. Teachers are best suited to talk to their students about the political process in ways they can understand and empower them to engage responsibly.

Teachers already wear many hats—educators, counselors, custodians, surrogate parents—and starting potentially controversial conversations might create even more work. It's easy to understand why some teachers, especially public school teachers, might balk at urging their students to skip school to protest, let alone joining the protest themselves. Considering a teacher was arrested at a January school board meeting for disagreeing with the board, it is not surprising that many teachers choose to keep their political views to themselves, even if they agree with their students' stance on gun control.

But no matter their views on the Second Amendment, teachers must use this opportunity to engage with their students on the First. Nothing drives home a lesson on the Constitution like putting it to use.

In addition to giving students a platform to use their constitutionally protected voices, the national school walkout offers a wealth of lessons on freedom of speech, civic responsibility, and the history and effectiveness of protest movements in the US. It is incumbent on every teacher in America to find ways to talk with their students about their rights and responsibilities in protest.

There are many ways for teachers to meet this challenge. If your school welcomes the idea of class discussion—or better still, school assembly—on the topic of gun violence, take a lead in organizing

Protests and other expressions of free speech can teach students about the First Amenedment.

one. If your district avoids political topics, consider hosting the discussion after school so as not to disrupt class schedules.

Consider teaming up with fellow teachers to coordinate your messaging and plans. There's strength in solidarity, and you can present a united front with fellow teachers and your students by wearing orange in support of the movement. Whatever your views on the content of the protests, this has an unparalleled potential for an experiential First Amendment lesson.

Assure your students that their personal views on gun control cannot be held against them, no matter where they stand in the debate, and that they all are entitled to join the conversation. If you need backup, print out a copy of the National Coalition Against Censorship's comic-illustrated guide for student protesters. Pop some corn and screen the American Civil Liberties Union's recent "Know Your Rights" video.

Make sure your students are aware of your school's absence policy and how it might affect them. Many university administrators have given assurances that suspensions will not be held against students pursuing admission. Still, you can show your students you support their right to free expression by offering to help them explain protest-related disciplinary actions on their applications.

Of course, for some students and some teachers, a walkout simply isn't a viable option. There's still plenty teachers can do to support their students in taking a stand for the issues they care about. If safety is an issue, teachers can ask students to brainstorm symbolic ways of protesting and let them vote on the top options. Whether students walk outside of their school or walk out into a hallway, the message behind their demonstration will be clear. They can also wear orange to show solidarity with the movement. The most important thing is that any action be student-led, inclusive, voluntary and peaceful.

Teachers can amplify their students' voices with pre-addressed letters to their elected officials and give them the chance to petition their demands either during class or at home.

Participation in—or abstention from, or counterprotest of—the national student walkout is protected speech. Wednesday's protests will present a momentous opportunity for students to exercise their First Amendment rights and take part in an important civic discourse. If the purpose of education is to prepare an informed and engaged citizenry, there may be no greater assignment this year.

EVALUATING THE AUTHOR'S ARGUMENTS:

The viewpoint author claims that staging a walkout is a protected right for students but does not detail the rights of schools to punish them if they perceive the event to be disruptive. She thus indicates that the desire to take action on an issue kids feel strongly about outweighs any negative consequences. How does this differ from the viewpoints you've read so far?

Student Protest Is as American as Apple Pie

Mark Keierleber

"Going back to the civil rights movement and beyond, courting danger has long been part of youth activism."

In the following excerpted viewpoint Mark Keierleber argues that student protest is a longstanding tradition in the United States. The author cites a landmark 1969 US Supreme Court case that involved a 13-year-old Iowa eighth grader who chose to wear a black armband in school to protest US involvement in Vietnam. He uses an interview with Mary Beth Tinker, who was one of the subjects of the case, to draw parallels between past and current events centering on the freedom of students to protest. Keierleber is a senior writer for The 74, a nonprofit website that focuses on issues of education.

AS YOU READ, CONSIDER THE FOLLOWING QUESTIONS:

1. What was *Tinker v. Des Moines*?
2. What is the "Tinker Standard" according to the viewpoint?
3. How did student protest bring about DACA?

"17 Minutes of History: Wednesday's Walkout Part of Long Tradition of Students Speaking Out, from *Tinker v. Des Moines* to Black Lives Matter," by Mark Keierleber, The 74 Media, Inc., March 13, 2018. Reprinted by permission.

Just days after a gunman walked onto campus and killed 17 people, Parkland, Florida, student Emma González took the podium in Fort Lauderdale with fervor. Seventeen classmates and teachers at Marjory Stoneman Douglas High School had been killed in one of America's deadliest school mass shootings and, in a high-profile speech to promote gun control measures, González offered a promise: Someday, their story would appear in textbooks.

"Just like *Tinker v. Des Moines*, we are going to change the law," González said, referring to the landmark Supreme Court decision that defined the First Amendment rights of public school students. "That's going to be Marjory Stoneman Douglas in that textbook and it's going to be due to the tireless effort of the school board, the faculty members, the family members, and—most of all—the students."

On Wednesday, the debate over gun control, student safety, and student free speech rights takes center stage as students from hundreds of schools across the country walk out of class to demand that Congress address gun violence in American schools. The 17-minute "National School Walkout" is one of several local and national student protests scheduled over the next month. Although the event is a response to a deadly school shooting, it's about more than that, as González suggested in her speech. It's also about students making their voices heard in policy debates that are often drowned out by adults, and their right to do so.

In an interview with The 74, the woman who helped define the free speech rights of public school students agreed that the Parkland students are making history.

"I think it may be a real turning point" in the gun debate, said Mary Beth Tinker, whose landmark Supreme Court victory in 1969 found that students do not "shed their constitutional rights to freedom of speech or expression at the schoolhouse gate."

The Tinker Standard

Five decades after Tinker wore a black armband to school in Des Moines, Iowa, to protest the Vietnam War, the retired nurse now travels to schools across the country and encourages students to speak up. "I was telling some kids, 'When the kids marched in Birmingham in 1963, Martin Luther King Jr. called it a turning point in the civil

Mary Beth Tinker and her brother John were suspended for wearing black armbands to protest the Vietnam War.

rights movement, and I think this is another turning point now," she said.

Tinker was referring to a campaign by King and the Southern Christian Leadership Conference to challenge racial discrimination in one of America's most segregated cities. As black students attempted to march downtown, hundreds were arrested. Then, at the direction of Commissioner of Public Safety Eugene "Bull" Connor—a notorious segregationist—the children were sprayed with high-pressure water hoses, beaten by police batons, and attacked by police dogs.

Even if they don't face the hardships of their civil rights–era forebears, today's student protesters face some risk, including potential punishment by school officials. Under the "Tinker standard," the Supreme Court found that educators can punish student speech if it's a substantial disruption to learning. And while schools may not be allowed to punish students for political statements, like a demand for gun control, First Amendment attorneys said student protesters could run into trouble for breaking other rules, such as truancy policies that prohibit students from cutting class.

Despite the Supreme Court ruling that students have First Amendment rights, student walkouts don't meet the "Tinker standard" threshold, said Esha Bhandari, a staff attorney with the

American Civil Liberties Union's Speech, Privacy, and Technology Project. Schools have the right to prohibit student absences, she said, even if those absences are politically motivated.

"I think the critical point here ... is that the punishment shouldn't be greater or harsher because of the nature of the absence being a political protest," she said. "Schools may be permitted to punish students for their actions—for not being in class—but they can't punish them for their ideas."

Disobedience & Consequences

As school districts across the country brace for a mass student exodus—if only for 17 minutes—the responses from administrators have varied. In New York City, student protesters will get a notation in the student attendance record for their civil disobedience but won't otherwise be punished. Other districts, including the Needville Independent School District in Texas, plan to suspend students who skip class.

In a Facebook post, Needville Superintendent [Curtis] Rhodes wrote that students who participate in the walkout will be suspended for three days and "face all the consequences that come along with an out of school suspension." He added, "Life is all about choices and every choice has a consequence whether it be positive or negative."

Ahead of Wednesday's national walkout, smaller protests have percolated in communities across the country, and schools have already punished students for ditching class. After a walkout in Scottsdale, Arizona, about 40 students received one-day suspensions for marching off campus.

If history means anything, that risk of school discipline could make their voices even stronger, said Frank LoMonte, director of the Brechner Center for Freedom of Information and an expert on student First Amendment rights. Going back to the civil rights movement and beyond, courting danger has long been part of youth activism.

"You have to be willing to put a little skin in the game but not cross the line to where you lose the public's sympathy and understanding," he said. "You can lock arms and sit in front of the college president's office, but you can't burn down the president's mansion."

Historical Parallels

Tinker sees parallels between the students pushing for gun control legislation and her own anti-war activism. Just like some of the more outspoken violence victims in Parkland, Tinker's family received death threats for speaking up. She was scrutinized for her age. As students began to advocate for gun control after the Parkland tragedy, conservative commentator Ben Shapiro argued that youth "are not fully rational actors." Others accused teens of being paid crisis actors. Bill O'Reilly, the ousted Fox News personality, accused national news outlets of using children as a prop to attack President Donald Trump.

Those are the same tactics that were used in 1965, Tinker said. The daughter of a Methodist minister, Tinker was a 13-year-old eighth-grader when she and other students wore black armbands to her Des Moines school to protest the Vietnam War. The students were promptly disciplined for violating a policy banning armbands. Meanwhile, community members criticized Tinker for her age, concluding she couldn't possibly know enough about Vietnam to have an informed opinion.

"But the fact is, most adults didn't know very much, at all, about Vietnam either," she said. "When young people are criticized just for the fact of their age, that just shows that people have a pretty weak critique of what's going on."

From the civil rights movement to anti-violence protests during the Vietnam War to the Black Lives Matter Movement, student voices have long been a driving force in advancing American social issues. Young voices have been crucial for "every progressive social movement," argues a recent Harvard University report. Though young people are often characterized as being disengaged or apathetic, according to the report, their actions have long had a powerful impact on American politics.

Nine months before Rosa Parks was arrested in Montgomery, Alabama, for refusing to give up her bus seat to a white person,

15-year-old Claudette Colvin was arrested for doing the same thing. In 1963, about half of Chicago's students walked out of class to protest a lack of resources for segregated black schools.

More recently, the Harvard paper noted, undocumented students staged sit-ins, including one at Sen. John McCain's office, to demand immigration reform. Those student actions eventually led the Obama administration to announce the Deferred Action for Childhood Arrivals program, also known as DACA, in 2012. When the Trump administration announced last fall it would end DACA, hundreds of Denver students marched out of school in protest.

Through Black Lives Matter protests, which began after the 2013 acquittal of the man who shot and killed teen Trayvon Martin, young people have mobilized to demand new gun laws and criminal justice reform.

The *Tinker* case can still be felt in the Des Moines area, said Iowa native Ian Coon, a student at Wartburg College and communications director for Student Voice, a student-led nonprofit that encourages students to speak up about school inequities. Recently, he said, student activism led officials to open inclusive bathrooms for transgender students at Des Moines's Roosevelt High School.

Student protests are often carried out by marginalized youth, but Coon said the students from Parkland, a well-off suburb, have had some advantages. The most vocal students from Parkland "come from home lives that allowed them to be advocates and not have to worry about surviving as people before they can use their voice, which has not always been seen in the past where it's the most marginalized speaking up for themselves."

EVALUATING THE AUTHOR'S ARGUMENTS:

How does the viewpoint author allow readers to form their own views on the rights of students to protest gun violence? How does comparing events of the past and the present help readers draw conclusions?

Student Protest Can Change the World

United Way of Greater Los Angeles

"They walked out despite school administrators barring doors. They walked out despite helmeted police officers wielding night sticks."

In the following viewpoint United Way of Greater Los Angeles compares the banding together of students fighting for gun control today to the formation of the Chicano Youth Leadership Conference in 1968. The authors argue that such movements gather strength through passion of an issue and a sense of togetherness. They recall the violence perpetrated against protesters and express hope that times have changed to the point in which negative reactions to modern-day student protesters will remain peaceful. The United Way fights for improved education, income, and health in communities around the world.

AS YOU READ, CONSIDER THE FOLLOWING QUESTIONS:

1. Why are the 1960s considered the peak of student protest activity in the United States?
2. Why was the violence against protesting students not made public?
3. On what charges were the East LA 13 arrested?

"The Walkout—How a Student Movement in 1968 Changed Schools Forever (Part 1 of 3)," United Way of Greater Los Angeles, February 26, 2018. Reprinted by permission.

It was the height of civil rights activism. Spring of 1968.

Five years prior, Martin Luther King, Jr., inspired a nation with his "I Have a Dream" speech on the steps of the Lincoln Memorial following the March on Washington. Not long after, the Civil Rights Act of 1964 became law. A year later in the Spring of 1965, more than 600 protesters marched from Selma to Montgomery, Alabama. A few months after that, the Voting Rights Act of 1965 would be signed into law.

Meanwhile, in Los Angeles County, the largest Latino community in the United States had more than 130,000 students attending area schools. And their prospects were dim. Graduation rates were one of the lowest in the country. The dropout rate at Garfield High School in East Los Angeles was a staggering 57.5%. Average class sizes in area schools were 40 students and the ratio of school counselors to students was one counselor to 4000 students.

Mexican-American students went on to have a college graduation rate of ~0.1%, often due to lack of access to college-readiness courses and lack of support from teachers and administrators who encouraged the students to not even try for college.

Put simply, the students were being held down.

The Spark of Inspiration

But a spark was lit in 1963. Sal Castro—a teacher at Lincoln High School in East Los Angeles, a Mexican-American, and an educator who worked to instill pride in his students' Chicano heritage—led the first Chicano Youth Leadership Conference at Camp Hess in Malibu. This conference would inspire and motivate a generation of leaders, including future Los Angeles Mayor Antonio Villaraigosa, California Supreme Court Associate Justice Carlos Moreno, and filmmaker Moctesuma Esparza.

But, first, it would be the catalyst for the 1968 walkouts.

Moctesuma Esparza—who first attended the Chicano Youth Leadership Conference in 1965, would be one of the primary organizers of the walkouts, and later produced an HBO film about the events—described the cultural climate during an interview with democracynow.org during the 2006 release of the Walkout film:

High school students in New York City protested the Vietnam War in 1966.

"This is 1967, while the Vietnam War is in full bore, and protests are growing, and the Civil Rights Movement is flourishing. And throughout the world, young people are looking to change the world. And this was not lost on the kids in East L.A. They were able to see what their own circumstances were and how they were being oppressed, how they were being denied an opportunity for an education, an opportunity to fulfill their lives. And so, it was not difficult to organize them."

From that political and social climate, this small collection of young college and high school students would come together under the leadership of their teacher, Sal Castro, to organize a series of walkouts elevating the needs of their community.

The Walkouts of 1968

It took six months of planning. The walkouts were coordinated to take place on March 6, 1968, at 10 a.m.

An event invite couldn't be created on Facebook. A viral video couldn't be uploaded to YouTube. A message couldn't be spread on Twitter. The students had to organize one-on-one. They had to plan after school and on the weekends. In between homework and jobs.

They built up support amongst East L.A. schools and the student bodies were ready. Maybe too ready. Because on Friday, March 1, students at Wilson High School walked out five days early in an impromptu protest of the cancellation of a student-produced play.

But this didn't stop the coordinated effort from coming together again on the planned March 6 walkouts. And again and again over the ensuing week. All told, an estimated 15,000 students walked out of classes from Woodrow Wilson, Garfield, Abraham Lincoln, Theodore Roosevelt, Belmont, Venice and Jefferson High Schools.

They walked out despite school administrators barring doors. They walked out despite helmeted police officers wielding night sticks. At the time, there were two reported cases of student beatings during the March 6 walkout at Roosevelt.

And, yet the violence was so much more extreme. Despite news outlets like CBS, NBC, and the *L.A. Times* being at the walkouts, the police violence toward the students was not covered in the media. Esparza recalled the violence during his interview with democracynow.org:

"These were high school kids who were peacefully protesting for their rights. They were children. And they were brutalized. There are blows that were recorded on film that were like death blows. It was really, really awful. And when that footage was finally discovered in 1995, when the research was being done for the PBS documentary *Chicano*, it was astonishing to us that that footage had survived and even existed."

Luis Garza, a photojournalist for La Raza at the time of the walkouts, saw firsthand what the students faced.

"You're going up against an authoritative system that allowed for no protests and would rather suppress it rather than engage in dialogue," he said. "So there were consequences."

"You have the LAPD. You have sheriffs. You have undercover surveillance. You have intimidation and threats that are being made," he continued. "You're being castigated and vilified for protesting for a subject that does not take into account who you are what you're trying to express."

The violence might have escaped popular attention, but the message of the students did not. Carrying signs, and many joined by family members, students brought greater light to the racism and marginalization happening in their schools. Their walkouts and message started to finally catch the attention of the school board.

But it took time.

"They were not concentrated into a day or a week," recalled Garza. "The evolution of those walkouts was a slow and steady process. People got arrested. People got indicted. People had to go to court. People spent jail time."

The Students Make Their Demands

On March 28, 1968, more than 1,200 community members came together in front of the Los Angeles Board of Education to support the students as they presented their demands.

But the Board denied their demands.

Three days later, 13 of the walkout organizers—later known as the East L.A. 13—were arrested for "conspiracy to disturb the peace." Protests took place outside the Hall of Justice in downtown Los Angeles calling for their release. It wasn't long before 12 of the 13 were released.

Sal Castro, the teacher who had inspired so many students to take pride in their heritage, remained held for much longer and later lost his teaching position at Lincoln High School. But thanks to round-the-clock sit-ins at the L.A. School Board office, Castro was given back his job and began teaching again.

While policies and schools didn't change at first, the students and community leaders never stopped advocating for change. Despite the arrests. Despite the initial denial of demands.

And, over time, things began to change.

Los Angeles schools started to see more Mexican-American administrators, more bilingual educators, and, eventually, superintendents. The 1970s saw significant increases in the number of Latinos attending colleges and universities across the nation.

But it would take 40 years for students in Los Angeles to gain their rights to college-readiness programs through district policies.

EVALUATING THE AUTHORS' ARGUMENTS:

The viewpoint authors state that changes in the Latino community took time to develop, but that calling attention to issues through protest can indeed create a better world. What do you infer from their viewpoint about today's students?

Chapter 2

Are Student Protesters Tolerant of Other Perspectives?

Some charge that demonstrators should be more respectful of the opposite side.

Free Expression Hostilities on Campus Originate with Liberals

"Are these incidents of political violence and harassment outliers or part of a growing trend of hostility towards free expression on campus?"

Preston Stovall

In the following viewpoint Preston Stovall utilizes strong research to analyze the issue of banning distasteful speakers on college campuses. The author cites events on individual campuses and national trends among students to band together against right-wing speakers to provide an overall look at the current situation. Stovall indicates that such issues are a reflection of modern polarization with Americans clashing over hard-right or hard-left views. Stovall is a postdoctoral researcher for Heterodox Academy, a politically diverse group of professors and graduate students that seek to improve the quality of research and teaching through the debating of wide-ranging views.

"Are Students Increasingly Hostile to Free Expression on Campus? Look to Behaviors, Not Surveys," by Preston Stovall, Heterodox Academy, August 13, 2018. Reprinted by permission.

1. How has social media changed the ways students can stage protests on campus?
2. Does the psychologist cited in this viewpoint provide predictions based on fact about the future of student protests?
3. Does this viewpoint prove that there is a serious threat to freedom of speech in American universities?

In the Berkeley protests against Milo Yiannopoulos in February of 2017, the so-called "black bloc" showed up to a vocal, but mostly peaceful, protest. They caused enough physical damage to buildings on campus that the University police backed off—giving the attackers free reign to destroy property, and ultimately leading to the cancelation of Yiannopoulos' talk. Since then, talks from Ben Shapiro and Ann Coulter have cost Berkeley nearly one million dollars to ensure the safety of the speakers and their audiences.

At a talk given by Charles Murray at Middlebury College in March of 2017, student protests sufficient to drown out the invited speaker turned violent as Murray and other faculty were assaulted when leaving the building.

At a political rally in Berkeley in April of 2017, a masked figure swung from behind a protester talking with a Trump supporter to strike the Trump supporter with a bike lock—with such force that it doubled him over and left a deep laceration on his head.

At Evergreen State College, a series of confrontations in 2017 led to barricaded rooms, the cancellation of classes across the entire university, roving bands of armed students, and a physical assault against defenders of Bret Weinstein who were using a "free speech zone."

At a talk given by Christina Hoff Sommers at the Lewis and Clark Law School in March of this year, student protesters attempted to shout down the speaker and the speaker-audience conversation.

Are these incidents of political violence and harassment outliers or part of a growing trend of hostility towards free expression on campus?

Violent protests have erupted on several university campuses over conservative speakers.

One popular way to explore this question has been through surveys gauging attitudes about free speech among contemporary youth. Heterodox Academy's Jon Haidt & Sean Stevens, FIRE's Nico Perrino, and Rutgers Psychology professor Lee Jussim and others have argued that major nationally-representative polls of students do suggest that a change may be underway, specifically among the generation of youth that San Diego State University psychologist Jean Twenge has dubbed "iGen."

However, by relying so heavily on polling to answer this question, both those who believe a major shift is underway and their detractors risk committing what sociologists Jerolmack & Khan dubbed the "attitudinal fallacy": What people say on polls may not accurately reflect or predict how they will behave "in the world." For instance, many who staunchly support free speech in the abstract may stand idly by in the face of attempts at suppressing controversial views on campus—or may even join in themselves.

To the extent that we are concerned about illiberal behaviors rather than attitudes, we should attempt to observe and catalog how people act over what they profess to believe.

Contemporary American college students live in an environment of 24/7 social media, mass-media, public displays of political allegiance, and the ability to record the world around them almost any time they wish.

These "open sources" can empower social scientists to develop and test hypotheses in ways that go beyond the polling of opinions—and ultimately develop fairly objective assessments on the relative propensity toward political violence and harassment among various factions, at least as recorded and disseminated by the students themselves.

Researchers could begin by focusing on events that:

- occur either on college campuses, or at events sponsored by student organizations
- involve the use of either physical violence or collective agency directed at keeping people from speaking (e.g. by shouting together to drown out a conversation)
- are driven by participants who have clearly aligned themselves with the political left or the political right

Sources of data for tracking these putative trends include video recordings, police records of arrests and convictions, news reports from multiple reliable sources, etc.

By building up a database of episodes which meet these conditions, we can develop a more accurate picture of the prevalence of political violence and political harassment on college campuses today—and make more fine-grained predictions about tendencies among those on the left and the right.

Predictions

If this author were to hypothesize on what would be found through an empirical study of this nature, in order of diminishing credence I would estimate:

- Evidence since 2015 will show that most contemporary incidents of harassment or intimidation at campus events originate with the left (using data from F.I.R.E., this trend was noted in an essay by Stevens and Haidt).
- Outside campus settings, we will see a tendency for organized events to draw both supporters and protesters who come

prepared for physical confrontation (think Antifa and the Proud Boys). In these settings it will be harder to determine whether violence tends to be due more to those on the left or on the right, though I suspect overall both sides will share close to the same responsibility.

- Campus incidents will be disproportionately clustered around small liberal arts colleges, and at universities in large urban centers in historically "blue" counties.

In terms of the trend going forward (again in order of diminishing credence):

- By fostering dialogue among various factions, and thereby promoting mutual understanding, we shall help cause the frequency and intensity of these incidents to decline.
- In 30 years it will be possible to look back on the contemporary college scene concerning freedom of expression in much the way we look at the turbulence on American college campuses in the 1960s and 70s—viz., a mostly productive response to genuine problems, interspersed with a bit of idealistic fanaticism rightly subject to criticism.

In conversation over an earlier draft of this essay Rutgers psychologist Lee Jussim offered me the following predictions (in no particular order):

- Conservatives in the social sciences and humanities are currently on the Endangered Species List—and will probably go extinct, at least at liberal arts and coastal colleges and universities over the next 20 years. Nonleftists (libertarians, moderates, etc.) are currently Vulnerable, and will probably move to Endangered. One need not wait 20 years to test; pre-registered prediction: % of each will continue to decline.
- Academics will far more frequently and forcefully denounce academics who write conservative essays/editorials than those who

write liberal ones. This would probably best be scaled against the overall # of left/right individuals or articles.

- Conservative students will feel more uncomfortable speaking up on campus than do liberals. This trend will continue and worsen.
- Scholarship will focus almost exclusively on questions that academics on the left want answered. If some field is 98% left, this becomes true almost by definition.
- An important limitation, I think, is that it will take years to do this sort of research. If so, doing it won't help cope with our current situation, regardless of whether or not we view it as a crisis (outlets on the left insist it isn't, outlets on the right insist it is).
- Faster solution than waiting years for the research? Survey moderates, independents, and libertarians. Treat them as, if not quite unbiased, at least less biased, actors. Pre-registered prediction: large majorities of such groups will say "yes, there is a serious problem."

EVALUATING THE AUTHOR'S ARGUMENTS:

Did Preston Stovall require a personal view to bring the issue of freedom of expression on college campuses into stark focus? He cites incidents of stifling potential speakers and the waging of verbal and even physical confrontations to call attention to a growing problem that threatens the inalienable American freedom of speech while alluding to the impact of social media.

Freedom of Expression Is Limited

Gene Policinski and Lata Nott

"While students have First Amendment rights, they are not as extensive as those enjoyed by adults."

In the following viewpoint Gene Policinski and Lata Nott argue that the right to free speech does not always pertain to public school students. The authors advise student protesters and their parents to inform themselves on their First Amendment rights and to weigh the importance of their fight against any repercussions that might come their way. Policinski is COO of the Freedom Forum Institute, which seeks to protect First Amendment rights. Nott is the organization's executive director.

AS YOU READ, CONSIDER THE FOLLOWING QUESTIONS:

1. What punishments are justified for those who harass fellow students for not participating in a walkout at school?
2. Do these authors show any favoritism in their views about student rights to stage protests?
3. How do the authors use the First Amendment to teach readers about the issue?

"School Walkouts in the Wake of 'Parkland'—Protected by the First Amendment or Not?," by Gene Policinski and Lata Nott, Freedom Forum Institute, February 22, 2018. Reprinted by permission.

The national walkouts that students are currently organizing to call for new gun control legislation are commendable examples of "Generation Z" exercising its First Amendment freedoms. Unfortunately, students, teachers and other staff are likely to run up against legal limits around free speech and protest on school grounds.

On March 14, exactly one month after the Feb. 14 shootings at Marjory Stoneman Douglas High School in Parkland, Fla., students, teachers and administrators across the nation plan to walk out of their classrooms at 10 a.m. in each time zone, for 17 minutes—one minute for each student and teacher killed in the attack. Another such event is scheduled for April 20, the 19th anniversary of the Columbine High School massacre in Colorado. More than 22,000 people have signed a petition pledging to walk out of their classrooms at 10 a.m. for the rest of the day.

While some school districts may support or sign on to these protests, others have already announced that they will not. Needville Independent School District, about 60 miles southwest of Houston, has threatened to suspend any students who participate in walkouts or other protests that happen during school hours.

Marches, walkouts and sit-ins are the embodiment of our core freedoms: the right to speak out, to assemble peaceably and petition our government for change. Such protests recall powerful moments in the civil rights movement, when energized groups of young people caught the nation's attention and successfully pushed for social and political change.

The student voices in the Parkland movement also call to mind the circumstances around the landmark 1969 Supreme Court decision *Tinker v. Des Moines Independent School District*, which also involved teens, schools and the freedom to protest.

In that case, the court considered a 1965 protest in which five students wore black armbands—one of which is on display at the Newseum, in Washington, DC—to protest the Vietnam War. Three older students were suspended by school authorities for defying instructions not to wear the armbands. Their parents filed a lawsuit and the Supreme Court found that this was a violation of the students' First Amendment rights. Justice Abe Fortas wrote that neither

While some schools permitted demonstrations during National Walkout Day, public schools did have the right to prohibit such participation.

students nor teachers "shed their constitutional rights to freedom of speech or expression at the schoolhouse gate."

But here's an early caution to those planning school walkouts and protests on school grounds: The *Tinker* decision and later court cases also ruled that while students have First Amendment rights, they are not as extensive as those enjoyed by adults. Their free expression rights can be curtailed by school officials if they can prove that the student action would "materially and substantially interfere" with education in the school, or interfere with the rights of others. In *Tinker*, the Supreme Court found that the three armband-wearing students could not be punished by school authorities because their silent protest did not significantly disrupt education in the school.

Would the same be true for students who participate in classroom walkouts? The answer is "it depends"—on district and state truancy policies, for example—because the courts have carved out exceptions to *Tinker*, citing the education mission of schools in comparison to society at large.

Heading into these protests, students, parents and teachers should all understand the lengths to which their actions are protected by the First Amendment.

- For students: If your school district does not allow for participation in the walkouts, you could face penalties and punishment for disrupting the school day, violating school rules and potentially (although less likely) for intruding on the rights of students who do not walk out of class that day. You may decide that you are willing to incur those penalties but remember to consider alternative methods of advocacy and protest as well. Sometimes civil disobedience—challenging the rules on matters of conscience and policy—is justifiable. But sometimes there are other ways to achieve the same goal.
- For parents: Take this opportunity to work collectively with other parents and your school leaders on the larger civic lessons around this growing youth movement.
- For school officials: You first face the decision of whether to forbid a walkout or to simply deal with the disruption caused by a walkout. (This decision might depend on whether students are planning a 17-minute walkout or an all-day walkout.) You then face the decision of whether or not to punish participants. Like the students, you should also consider that there may be another approach altogether. It is possible—perhaps in cooperation with students and parents—to turn the event into a teaching moment, in which all sides around the contentious, long-standing gun control debate are heard.

Given that we live in an age where there is much concern that young people don't understand the Constitution or support free speech, punishing them for exercising it seems counterproductive, even if the *Tinker* decision does give school administrators that ability. Holding discussions in advance of the protests, using NewseumED's resources on student speech, petition and advocacy, can help students understand how democracy and representative government work, and become active and effective participants in civil society.

Perhaps Needville ISD Superintendent Curtis Rhodes will consider such a "teaching moment." A few days ago, Rhodes sent a letter to parents, saying the district "will not allow a student demonstration during school hours for any type of protest or awareness" and threatening suspensions and other "consequences."

"A school is a place to learn and grow educationally, emotionally and morally," Rhodes said in a Facebook post that has since been removed. "A disruption of the school will not be tolerated ... We are here for an education and not a political protest."

Note to Rhodes: Political protest is a part of the history and governing process of the United States, from the Boston Tea Party protests to modern-day Tea Party marches and much more. It's a part of Texas history too. Consider the Conventions of 1832 and 1833, where future Texans gathered to seek a rollback of laws and taxes imposed by the then-ruling Mexican government.

In other words, how about a little less "sit down" in response to the planned student walkout, and a little more "let's talk" about the importance of citizen engagement in a democracy.

EVALUATING THE AUTHORS' ARGUMENTS:

How have the experiences of the two viewpoint authors writing about the First Amendment given them the ideal background to tackle this issue? Why is it important for student protesters to know the law and their constitutional rights?

Attempts to Protect Free Speech on Campus Might Inhibit It

"Institutions shouldn't seek to restrict students' First Amendment speech rights to strict borders on campus."

Neal H. Hutchens

In the following viewpoint Neal H. Hutchens argues that institutions of learning should be allowed to create a non-disruptive atmosphere on their campuses but are going too far. He gives mixed reviews to proposed legislature, such as a bill promoted by Wisconsin lawmakers that would ensure that speakers with whom protesting students disagree cannot be silenced. He applauds that attempt but believes the result would be an unfortunate stifling of protest and force schools to decide what forms are punishable and which are not. Hutchens is a professor of higher education at the University of Mississippi.

"New Legislation May Make Free Speech on Campus Less Free," by Neal H. Hutchens, The Conversation, 04/27/2017. https://theconversation.com/new-legislation-may-make-free-speech-on-campus-less-free-77609. Licensed under CC BY-ND 4.0.

AS YOU READ, CONSIDER THE FOLLOWING QUESTIONS:
1. What are the arguments for and against free speech zones on campuses?
2. What role does the ACLU have in issues regarding student protests?
3. Should the Wisconsin State Assembly bill protecting speakers from disruption on college campuses apply to those who promote hate against racial or sexual minorities?

Around the country, state lawmakers have been talking about—and legislating—ways intended to protect free speech on college campuses.

The Wisconsin State Assembly, for example, recently passed a campus speech bill that would require public colleges and universities to punish students who disrupt campus speakers. The legislation is now heading to the State Senate for consideration.

As a higher education law researcher and campus free speech supporter, I view some requirements in these new campus speech laws as positively reinforcing legal protections for student free speech. However, I believe language in several pending state bills, including the punitive legislation proposed in Wisconsin, does more to impede free speech than protect it.

Free Speech Zones

In an effort to keep campuses safe and avoid disruption, some universities have restricted student speech and expressive activity—such as handing out leaflets or gathering signatures for petitions—to special speech zones.

These "free speech zones" have been subject to criticism and legal challenges. In one illustrative case, a federal court invalidated a University of Cincinnati policy that limited student demonstrations, picketing and rallies to one small portion of campus.

The US Supreme Court, however, has not ruled definitively on the legality of designated student speech zones. Consequently, legal battles over their constitutionality continue, as shown by pending

Some US lawmakers have tried to push legislation that would punish student protesters, an action that many consider un-American.

litigation involving a Los Angeles community college student who claims he was allowed to distribute copies of the US Constitution only in a designated campus speech zone.

Some states have recently enacted laws that prohibit public colleges and universities from enforcing such free speech zones against students. At least seven states have passed anti-speech zone laws: Virginia, Missouri, Arizona, Colorado, Tennessee, Utah and Kentucky.

Public institutions in these states may impose reasonable rules to avoid disruption, but officials cannot relegate student free speech and expression to only small or remote areas on campus. Instead, they must permit free speech in most open campus locations, such as courtyards and sidewalks.

Along with the pending legislation in Wisconsin, which also would ban speech zones, North Carolina, Michigan, Texas and Louisiana are considering similar legislation.

Striking down these "free speech zones" seems a sensible way to promote student free speech: In my opinion, institutions shouldn't seek to restrict students' First Amendment speech rights to strict borders on campus.

Punishing Protesters

If the Wisconsin bill passes in its current form, the state would do more than ban designated free speech zones. It would also become the first state requiring institutions to punish student protesters. The North Carolina House of Representatives has passed a similar bill, now under review in the State Senate, but this legislation seems to leave institutions more discretion over dealing with students disrupting speakers than the Wisconsin legislation.

Much of the push for campus speech bills has come from lawmakers who believe that college campuses are hostile to conservative speakers. They point to incidents such as those involving Ann Coulter and Milo Yiannopoulos at the University of California at Berkeley as indicative of an overall resistance to conservative speakers on campus.

Provisions in campus speech bills, including ones mandating penalties for students who disrupt speakers, can largely be traced to model legislation from the Goldwater Institute, based in Phoenix, Arizona. The group aims to correct what it views as a left-leaning bias in American higher education regarding campus free speech.

In my view, forcing colleges to take punitive action against all disruptive protesters is troublesome. Such a requirement would mean that institutions would be faced with devising overly cumbersome rules for when punishment should or should not occur. But what counts as a punishment-worthy disruption?

A more problematic outcome would be if free speech were chilled. Students might understandably refrain from speech and expressive activity based on fear of punishment, particularly if the rules around such punishment are necessarily vague and difficult to understand.

Based on such concerns, the Foundation for Individual Rights in Education—an influential group that promotes, among other things, student free speech in higher education—has come out against this particular requirement in the Wisconsin bill. The American Civil Liberties Union has also expressed concern over the similar provision under consideration in North Carolina.

Moving Forward

The Wisconsin bill is described by supporters as intended to protect the right of campus speakers to be heard. However, it seeks to accomplish this goal in a way that undermines student free speech of all types.

Hopefully, lawmakers in Wisconsin and in other states considering legislation will stick to workable measures that actually promote—as opposed to hinder—campus free speech.

EVALUATING THE AUTHOR'S ARGUMENTS:

How balanced is the assessment provided by the viewpoint author of how individual states are dealing with the issue of freedom of speech on college campuses?

Free Speech Doesn't Have to Include Hate Speech

Becca DiPietro

"Expending university resources to invite and actively promote a speaker of hate is wrong."

In the following viewpoint Becca DiPietro argues that there is a distinct difference between advocating free speech and tolerating hate speech. The author contends that college campuses are places to promote tolerance and diversity. She therefore believes that, while legal, inviting and promoting those who eschew those ideals is counterproductive to the well-being of students and a positive learning environment. DiPietro is a graduate of Georgetown University and served as an intern at the Center for American Progress.

AS YOU READ, CONSIDER THE FOLLOWING QUESTIONS:

1. How does the author draw a line between banning hate speech and inviting those who spew it on campus?
2. Is there a problem when most students believe free speech is secure on their campuses but also claim that their schools have done well in banning perceived offensive speakers?
3. Can healthy debate and discussion flourish on campuses in this contentious era of political discourse?

"There's a World of Difference Between Free Speech and Hate Speech," by Becca DiPietro, Center for American Progress, April 21, 2017. Reprinted by permission.

The recent appearance of a controversial speaker at Georgetown University, where I'm a student, bubbled over into a communitywide debate that pitted the social merits of free speech against the harm of hate speech.

Nonie Darwish, a prominent anti-Islam writer and speaker who has called for the annihilation of Islam, appeared at a forum sponsored by the Georgetown University College Republicans, or GUCR, to promote her new book. The event sparked divisive debate on campus, as many progressive students condemned the GUCR for giving Darwish a platform to spew her hateful views. The controversy even prompted a member of the GUCR board to resign in protest of Darwish's appearance.

Despite angry protests, however, the event proceeded and Darwish spoke. But the controversy didn't remain confined to campus. Local and national media chimed in to attack pro-Muslim students for protesting. To be honest, I was surprised that what seemed to only be important to students at my school mushroomed into a much larger issue and received such attention. However, I now understand that what happened at Georgetown serves as just one example of many similar conversations occurring at universities across the country. I do not believe that colleges should censor all hate speech by individuals, but expending university resources to invite and actively promote a speaker of hate is wrong.

Free Speech vs. Hate Speech

Universities should not censor any individual's speech, but they should acknowledge the roots of biases. Officials with the American Civil Liberties Union make this point:

> *Bigoted speech is symptomatic of a huge problem in our country; it is not the problem itself. Everybody, when they come to college, brings with them the values, biases and assumptions they learned while growing up in society, so it's unrealistic to think that punishing speech is going to rid campuses of the attitudes that gave rise to the speech in the first place. Banning bigoted speech won't end bigotry, even*

if it might chill some of the crudest expressions. The mindset that produced the speech lives on and may even reassert itself in more virulent forms.

While individual speech should be protected, however, university-sponsored speaker events differ from individual rights of free expression. Universities should be cognizant of not expending their resources on individuals who discriminate against members of their student bodies and encompass the antithesis of diversity, tolerance, and acceptance. After all, if universities serve to enrich the minds of society's young people, then how would a speaker of hate benefit anyone's education?

In addition to the protest at Georgetown, recent protests regarding controversial speakers have occurred at the University of California, Berkeley, and Middlebury College, among others. In each case, news stories highlight an ongoing public debate that pits free speech against hate speech. Even politicians have joined in the arguments, with some conservatives waging a war on so-called political correctness. They state that those who protest hate speech are ultimately promoting censorship as a means of controlling and avoiding speech with which they do not agree—speech that is free under the Constitution.

The idea of censorship is troubling but painting the anti-hate speech movement as part of an attempt to ignore reality avoids its nuance. Confronting hate speech is not about controlling the conversation but rather about promoting tolerance and inclusivity. And contrary to the sensationalized attention that the issue receives in the media, most college students do not feel that the anti-hate movement puts their right to free speech under attack.

A recent study by Gallup, the Knight Foundation, and the Newseum Institute found that 73 percent of college students think that their right to free speech is "very secure or secure." Moreover, a majority—71 percent—of students believe that policies universities have adopted "to discourage speech and behavior that could be seen as offensive or insensitive toward certain groups" have "been about right." Interestingly, 41 percent of black students felt that their college had "not gone far enough," while only 15 percent of white

Conservative speaker Milo Yiannopoulos was driven from the campus of the University of California, Berkeley.

students agreed. This gap shows that black students likely feel more of an impact when colleges work to prevent hateful expressions, such as racial slurs. The anti-hate speech movement seeks to help these students. While I don't advocate for policies that restrict individuals' rights of free speech, the underlying theme of these policies—when applied to university-sponsored events—demonstrates a goal of compassion and understanding.

Hate speech, when actively promoted by a university, is outside the bounds of free speech and should therefore exist beyond political sides. On the other hand, both sides should be wary of censorship. Unfortunately, however, the issue of speech on college campuses has become politicized and exaggerated.

Fostering Growth, Tolerance, and Understanding

Students who protest university-sponsored events that they view are promoting hateful speech are often criticized for being unwilling to hear the other side's opinion. The idea that students work to suppress the views of others ironically works to delegitimize those students' views and concerns in favor of perpetuating the problems of racism, sexism, homophobia, xenophobia, and Islamophobia.

There is no gold standard for distinguishing between hate speech and difference of opinion. Healthy, productive discussions are necessary to foster growth, tolerance, and understanding. Universities should try more to invite speakers who bring opinions that do not ostracize groups of people or religions but instead provide rational arguments based in truth. It is important that universities do not censor individuals' speech—even if some may consider that speech offensive. But it isn't conducive to learning for a university to actively promote and support bigoted ideas by inviting speakers known for their hateful, unsubstantiated views.

I question why the GUCR chose to invite someone without any academic credentials on her subject but known for her anti-Islam views. And I further wonder why the group chose to continue with its event after Muslim students and their allies pleaded against it. Perhaps the greatest challenge in issues such as this is how often the line between free speech and hate speech gets blurred. But by considering the debate in two different lights—one being censorship and the other being university-promoted speech—as well as by depoliticizing the issue, an attitude of empathy can be possible. Critics of protesters' pleas should step back and evaluate the roots of students' grievances and the roots of the hateful opinions rather than delegitimize students' concerns and desire for safe, welcoming environments. Why must there be a free speech and hate speech side? Why can't there simply be respect? Empathy for these very real feelings can make Georgetown and other universities what they should be— positive places for all students to debate and learn respectfully.

EVALUATING THE AUTHOR'S ARGUMENTS:

Viewpoint author Becca DiPietro strongly expresses her view that schools should not invite those considered intolerant and hateful onto their campuses, but does not specify where the line should be drawn between what is hate speech and what is simply conservative and acceptable. Would proposing such specifics strengthen the author's viewpoint, or is her argument sufficient as it stands?

Campuses Are for Open Minds

"This polarised image of vulnerable victims needing protection from vilified perpetrators is hardly a promising basis for a mature and respectful exchange of views on campus."

Jonathan Haidt and Nick Haslam

In the following viewpoint Jonathan Haidt and Nick Haslam argue that freedom of speech has been threatened by the mindset and attitude of many students and school administrations on American campuses. They assert that they have grown oversensitive as they seek to ban what they consider undesirable speakers at their schools. They cite the backlash over a simple chalked sign at Emory University that expressed support for Donald Trump during the 2016 presidential campaign as evidence that irrationality and a sense of victimization have needlessly and dangerously limited free speech. Haidt is professor of business and ethics at New York University Stern School of Business. Haslam is professor at the School of Psychological Sciences in Melbourne, Australia.

AS YOU READ, CONSIDER THE FOLLOWING QUESTIONS:

1. How has the Donald Trump presidency changed political discourse among American high school and college students?
2. Have bullies and racists felt more freedom to express themselves in the United States?
3. How have the authors cited the concept of positive diversity as under threat on college campuses?

Last month, in the early hours, an act of traumatising racist violence occurred on the campus of Emory University in Atlanta, Georgia. Students woke up to find that someone had written, in chalk, the words "Trump 2016" on various pavements and walls around campus. "I think it was an act of violence," said one student. "I legitimately feared for my life," said another; "I thought we were having a KKK rally on campus." Dozens of students met the university president that day to demand that he take action to repudiate Trump and to find and punish the perpetrators. Writing political statements in chalk is a common practice on American college campuses and, judging from the public reaction to the Emory event, most Americans consider the writing to be an act of normal free speech during the national collective ritual of a presidential election. So how did it come to pass that many Emory students felt victimised and traumatised by innocuous and erasable graffiti?

Emory students are not unique. Many other universities have been rocked by protests this year over what seem like small things to outsiders, such as Halloween costumes, dining hall food and sombreros. This new way of looking at things is spreading rapidly in the UK, too, with growing student demands for bans on words, ideas, speakers and, once again, sombreros. Students on both sides of the Atlantic are demanding that their campuses be turned into "safe spaces" where a subset of ideas and identities will not be challenged. What on earth is going on?

Part of the answer can be found in cultural shifts that have changed the meanings of many words and concepts used on campus,

Universities should be places where students can open their minds to new ideas. But does that include speech that is harmful?

making it hard for people off campus to understand what the protest-ers are saying. One of us (Haslam) recently published an essay titled "Concept Creep: Psychology's Expanding Concepts of Harm and Pathology." Many concepts are "creeping"—they are being "defined down" so that they are applied promiscuously to milder and less objectionable events.

Take bullying. When research on bullying began in the 1970s, an act had to meet four criteria to count: it had to be an act of aggression directed by one or more children against another child; the act had to be intentional; it had to be part of a repeated pattern; and it had to occur in the context of a power imbalance. But over the following decades, the concept of bullying has expanded in two directions.

It has crept outward or "horizontally" to encompass new forms of bullying, such as among adults in the workplace or via social media. More problematic, though, is the creeping downward or "vertically" so that the bar has been lowered and more minor events now count as bullying. For example, the criteria of intentionality and repetition are often dropped. What matters most is the subjective perception of the victim. If a person believes that he or she has been made to suffer in any way, by a single action, the victim can call it bullying. As the definition of bullying creeps downward for researchers, it also creeps downward in school systems, most of which now enforce strict anti-bullying policies. This may explain why Emory students, raised since elementary school with expansive notions of bullying and subjective notions of victimhood, could perceive the words "Trump 2016" as an act of bullying, intimidation, perhaps even violence, regardless of the intentions of the writer.

A second key concept that has crept downward is trauma. Medicine and psychiatry once reserved that word for physical damage to organs and tissues, such as a traumatic brain injury. But by the 1980s, events that caused extreme terror, such as rape or witnessing atrocities in war, were recognised as causing long-lasting effects known as post-traumatic stress disorder (PTSD).

The original criteria for PTSD required that a traumatic event "would evoke significant symptoms of distress in almost everyone" and would be "outside the range of usual human experience." But in recent trauma scholarship these stringent criteria are gone; like bullying, trauma is now assessed subjectively. In one recent definition used by a US Government agency, trauma refers to anything that is "experienced by an individual as physically or emotionally harmful or threatening and that has lasting adverse effects on the individual's functioning and physical, social, emotional, or spiritual well-being." For Emory students raised within a psychotherapeutic culture that employs this low threshold, we cannot blame them for labelling their reactions to "Trump 2016" as a personal and collective trauma. "We are in pain," said one of the students.

A third key campus concept that has crept downward is prejudice. As overt prejudice has declined precipitously, the term has crept outward and downward. For example, the concept of "modern racism" was developed to refer to people who may show no overt prejudice, but who endorse policy positions that might be associated with prejudice, such as opposing the use of racial preferences in college admissions. More recently, the concept of "implicit prejudice" has become popular after experiments showed that it takes most people slightly longer to associate pictures of Black people (vs. White people) with good words (vs. bad words).

As with bullying, prejudice is now in the eye of the beholder. If a person feels that a word, facial expression or even a subtle hand movement makes them uncomfortable in a way related to a protected identity, then an act of prejudice has occurred. For Emory students steeped in training about prejudice and inclusion, there is no need to know the intentions of the midnight chalker. The word "Trump" activates associations to racism in their minds. Therefore, anyone who writes his name has committed an act of racism, perhaps even traumatizing racial violence.

Concept creep does not happen to all psychological terms—it happens primarily to those that are useful in what sociologists have called a "culture of victimhood."

In such cultures there are two main sources of social prestige: being a victim or standing up for victims. But victimhood cultures don't emerge in the most racist or sexist environments—they tend to emerge in institutions that are already highly egalitarian (such as Emory and Yale) and in which there are authorities (such as deans and college presidents) that can be entreated to step in on the side of the victims. In such settings political potency is increased by amplifying the number of victims and the degree of their victimization. Concept creep serves as a rhetorical weapon of victimhood culture.

Once you understand this campus dynamic, you can more easily understand the many new concepts that have emerged from university campuses in the last few years.

If all of society, including the campus, is rife with bullying and prejudice, and if people are easily traumatised, then it is obviously a good and humane thing to provide members of marginalised groups with safe spaces where nobody will say things that might make them feel more marginalised. Some students want their entire campus to become a safe space, even if that means that non-progressive or non-approved ideas, professors and speakers are banned or denied a platform on the grounds that their words are considered hate speech. Advocates of "no platforming" will sometimes shout down speakers they disapprove of, denying everyone in the audience the chance to listen to a speaker they have come to hear.

The yearning for safety in a dangerous world also explains the growing demands that students make for trigger warnings, which are warnings professors are expected to give about any course readings that might activate memories of trauma in any of the students.

And it's not only reminders of rape that are triggering; students sometimes demand trigger warnings for novels that portray racism, classism or colonialism. It is everyone's collective duty to protect vulnerable students from experiencing negative emotions in the classroom. Those who want to lower the bar for definitions of bullying, trauma and prejudice hope that the expansion of these concepts will protect vulnerable people and raise the public's sensitivity to harm.

Regrettably, the outcomes are likely to be less rosy. Diluting concepts of harm swells the ranks of people who are encouraged to see themselves as harmed, vulnerable and in need of protection, which may cancel out any benefits gained by reducing insensitive behaviour.

As the Canadian philosopher Ian Hacking observed, concepts create identities. Hacking described "looping effects" in which people come to see themselves through the lens of a new concept and define themselves in its terms.

Students who are taught to interpret small or ambiguous experiences on campus, such as seeing "Trump 2016," as instances of bullying, trauma or prejudice, rather than as the ordinary ferment of differing people with differing views, come to see themselves as aggrieved and fragile victims. Their vulnerability defines them and gives them a moral platform from which to demand protection and safety. At the same time, they typecast their opponents as bullies, traumatisers and aggressors.

This polarised image of vulnerable victims needing protection from vilified perpetrators is hardly a promising basis for a mature and respectful exchange of views on campus. It shuts down free speech and the marketplace of ideas. And it is not even healthy for the students who are the objects of concern.

Of course young people need to be protected from some kinds of harm, but overprotection is harmful, too, for it causes fragility and hinders the development of resilience.

As Nasim Taleb pointed out in his book *Antifragile*, muscles need resistance to develop, bones need stress and shock to strengthen and the growing immune system needs to be exposed to pathogens in order to function. Similarly, he noted, children are by nature anti-fragile— they get stronger when they learn to recover from setbacks, failures and challenges to their cherished ideas.

A university that tries to protect students from words, ideas, and graffiti that they find unpleasant or even disgusting is doing them no favors. It is setting them up for greater suffering and failure when they leave the university and enter the workplace. Tragically, the very students who most need the strength to face later discrimination are the ones rendered weakest by victimhood culture on campus.

The unrest on university campuses has not just been caused by creeping concepts. Black and Muslim students, in particular, must endure ignorant questions and other indignities that other students rarely face. Diversity is difficult, and more must be done to make all feel welcome on campus. But universities should be careful not to encourage victimhood culture, looping effects and greater fragility.

One step that might reverse concept creep is to expand notions of diversity to include viewpoint diversity, especially political diversity. Between 1990 and 2010, American university faculties went from leaning left to being almost entirely on the left, especially in the humanities and social sciences. But if students are not exposed to conservative ideas, they are more likely to find them traumatising when they encounter them outside of college.

Ultimately, it is the students themselves who will have to stand up and reject victimhood culture and its creeping concepts. One way to do this is to embrace the term "danger" the way earlier activists reclaimed the term "queer."

Students at every university should push their student governments to hold a vote on whether the students want a "safe" university that routinely bans speakers, warns students about novels, and punishes students and professors for speech acts, or a "dangerous" university that takes no steps to protect its students from exposure to words, speakers, and ideas (with limited exceptions such as slander or threats of violence).

The debates that would surround such campus votes would help students see that too much safety is, ultimately, more dangerous than anything written in chalk.

EVALUATING THE AUTHORS' ARGUMENTS:

Viewpoint authors Jonathan Haidt and Nick Haslam make strong arguments about the dangers of weakening the rights of all students to express themselves without fear of reprisal or claims of prejudice. Do you think they have considered how minority students might feel marginalized and targeted on college campuses?

Chapter 3

Is Violence Ever Justified?

Antifa demonstrators were prepared for violence in their counterattack of alt-Right participants in the "Unite the Right" rally.

A Defense of Nonviolent Protest

"Nonviolent resistance is more effective than armed resistance in leading to more democratic societies."

John Dear

In the following viewpoint John Dear refutes civil rights activist Malcolm X's view that nonviolent protest is only good when it works, arguing instead that it is always the best tactic. The author bases his claim on several historical facts, including one from Nazi Germany in which Christian wives of Jewish men forced the repressive regime to return their husbands from captivity. Dear uses research from a book that explores the benefits of nonviolent civil resistance to back up his arguments. Dear is an activist, lecture, and author of 30 books, including *The Nonviolent Life*.

AS YOU READ, CONSIDER THE FOLLOWING QUESTIONS:

1. Does the message that nonviolence is fine if it works imply that that there is a time and place for violent protest?
2. How does the book cited in this viewpoint support the idea that nonviolence is always a superior form of protest?
3. Does the viewpoint author express an opinion on the superiority of nonviolent protest?

"The Facts Are In: Nonviolent Resistance Works," by John Dear, The National Catholic Reporter Publishing Company, October 16, 2012. Reprinted with permission of National Catholic Reporter Publishing Company, Kansas City, MO. NCRonline.org.

Nonviolence is fine as long as it works," Malcolm X once said. Recently, Columbia University Press published an extraordinary scholarly book that proves how nonviolence works far better as a method for social change than violence. This breakthrough book demonstrates that Gandhi was right, that the method of nonviolent resistance as a way to social change usually leads to a more lasting peace while violence usually fails.

Why Civil Resistance Works: The Strategic Logic of Nonviolent Conflict by Erica Chenoweth and Maria J. Stephan uses graphs, charts, sociological research and statistical analysis to show how in the last century, nonviolent movements were far better at mobilizing supporters, resisting regime crackdowns, creating new initiatives, defeating repressive regimes and establishing lasting democracies. Their evidence points to the conclusion that nonviolent resistance is more effective than armed resistance in overturning oppressive and repressive regimes and in leading to more democratic societies.

This report should cause the whole world to stop in its tracks and take up nonviolent conflict resolution and nonviolent resistance to injustice instead of the tired, old, obsolete methods of war and violence.

Why Civil Resistance Works is the first systematic study of its kind and takes us well beyond the research of Gene Sharp and others to demonstrate once and for all the power of nonviolent civil resistance for positive social change. Anyone interested in the methodology of nonviolent conflict resolution should get this book and study it. Indeed, one wishes the State Department and the government would learn its lessons, renounce its violence and start supporting nonviolent, people-power movements.

For more than a century, from 1900 to 2006, campaigns of nonviolent resistance were "more than twice as effective as their violent counterparts in achieving their stated goals," the authors conclude. By attracting widespread popular support through protests, boycotts, civil disobedience and other forms of nonviolent noncooperation, these campaigns broke repressive regimes and brought major new changes for justice and peace. Much of the book focuses on four case studies to explain their conclusions: the Iranian revolution of 1977–1979; the first Palestinian Intifada of 1987–92; the Philippines

Rev. Martin Luther King Jr. preached nonviolence as a way to achieve equality during the civil rights era.

People Power revolution of 1983–1986; and the Burmese uprising of 1988–90.

Through their statistical analysis, the authors found that non-violent resistance presents "fewer obstacles to moral and physical involvement and commitment, and that higher levels of participation contribute to enhanced resilience, greater opportunities for tactical innovation and civic disruption (and therefore less incentive for a regime to maintain its status quo), and shifts in loyalty among opponents' supporters, including members of the military establishment."

Contrary to popular belief, "violent insurgency is rarely justifiable on strategic grounds," they write. "Nonviolent resistance ushers in more durable and internally peaceful democracies, which are less likely to regress into civil war."

"We analyze 323 violent and nonviolent resistance campaigns between 1990 and 2006," the authors explain in their introduction.

> *Among them are over one hundred major nonviolent campaigns since 1900, whose frequency has increased over time. In addition to their growing frequency, the success*

rates of nonviolent campaigns have increased. How does this compare with violent insurgencies? One might assume that the success rates may have increased among both nonviolent and violent insurgencies. But in our data, we find the opposite: although they persist, the success rates of violent insurgencies have declined. The most striking finding is that between 1900 and 2006, nonviolent resistance campaigns were nearly twice as likely to achieve full or partial success as their violent counterparts. Among the 323 campaigns in the case of anti-regime resistance campaigns, the use of a nonviolent strategy has greatly enhanced the likelihood of success ... This book investigates the reasons why—in spite of conventional wisdom to the contrary—civil resistance campaigns have been so effective compared with their violent counterparts.

While only one in four violent campaigns succeed, about three out of four nonviolent campaigns succeed, they report. "We argue that nonviolent campaigns fail to achieve their objectives when they are unable to overcome the challenge of participation, when they fail to recruit a robust, diverse, and broad-based membership that can erode the power base of the adversary and maintain resilience in the face of repression."

The evidence of their research points to the superiority of nonviolent resistance at every level, including against genocidal regimes. "The claim that nonviolent resistance could never work against genocidal foes like Adolf Hitler and Joseph Stalin is the classic straw man put forward to demonstrate the inherent limitations of this form of struggle," they note.

While it is possible that nonviolent resistance could not be used effectively once genocide has broken out in full force, this claim is not backed by any strong empirical evidence. Collective nonviolent struggle was not used with any strategic forethought during World War II, nor was it ever contemplated as an overall strategy for resisting the Nazis. Violent resistance, which some groups attempted for ending Nazi occupation, was also an abject failure.

However, scholars have found that certain forms of collective nonviolent resistance were, in fact, occasionally successful in resisting Hitler's occupation policies. The case of the Danish population's resistance to German occupation is an example of partially effective civil resistance in an extremely difficult environment.

The famous case of the Rosenstrasse protests, when German women of Aryan descent stood for a week outside a detention center on the Rosenstrasse in Berlin demanding the release of their Jewish husbands, who were on the verge of being deported to concentration camps, is a further example of limited gains against a genocidal regime brought about by civil resistance. The German women, whose numbers increased as the protests continued and they attracted more attention, were sufficiently disruptive with their sustained nonviolent protests that the Nazi officials eventually released their Jewish husbands ... The notion that nonviolent action can be successful only if the adversary does not use violent repression is neither theoretically nor historically substantiated.

These studies "call for scholars to rethink power and its sources in any given society or polity," the authors suggest. "Our findings demonstrate that power actually depends on the consent of the civilian population, consent that can be withdrawn and reassigned to more legitimate or more compelling parties ... We hope that this book challenges the conventional wisdom concerning the effectiveness of nonviolent struggle and encourages scholars and policy makers to take seriously the role that civilians play in actively prosecuting conflict without resorting to violence."

I have long believed that Gandhi—and Jesus—were right to insist on the method of nonviolent resistance for both moral and practical reasons, but now the facts are in. The evidence is all laid out in this scholarly report.

The book went to press just as the revolutions of the Arab Spring were beginning. "If these last several months have taught us anything, it is that nonviolent resistance can be a near-unstoppable force for change in our world, even in the most unlikely circumstances." This book is a great resource for those of us who teach and advocate peace and nonviolence. More, it is a source of hope proving the ancient wisdom that mobilized nonviolent resistance is the best weapon for peaceful change. May it be taught far and wide and inspire many more to join the grassroots nonviolent movements for a new world of justice and peace.

EVALUATING THE AUTHOR'S ARGUMENTS:

Viewpoint author John Dear cites the success of nonviolent protests throughout history. Do you agree that nonviolence is always the solution to forcing positive change, or does it fail to promote constructive action? Explain your views.

Viewpoint

2

There Is Justifiable Violence

Christopher J. Finlay

> "One of the thorniest is the question of what the word 'violence' actually refers to."

In the following viewpoint Christopher J. Finlay relates the violence associated with the American Revolution to the protest violence some promote in the United States today. He notes that violence should generally be avoided but should not be ruled out as a way to ensure self-defense against extremist groups that threaten physical harm. Finlay uses historical evidence, such as the revolution in South Africa that dismantled apartheid, to argue that violence can be used to bring justice. Finlay is a professor of political theory at Durham University in England.

AS YOU READ, CONSIDER THE FOLLOWING QUESTIONS:
1. How does the author's definition of violence differ from what is generally accepted?
2. Is violence only in self-defense promoted in this article?
3. How does the author use a historical context to make his case for occasional violent protest?

"Is Violent Political Protest Ever Justified?" by Christopher J. Finlay, The Conversation, March 29, 2017. https://theconversation.com/is-violent-political-protest-ever-justified-72630. Licensed under CC BY-ND 4.0.

The mass protests against Donald Trump's election, inauguration, and executive actions might subside—but based on the scale and intensity of what's already happened, there's probably more to come.

So far, most protesters have limited themselves to marching, placard-waving, and other "peaceful" methods. There has, however, been some violence, and some demonstrators have adopted "disruptive" methods that fall somewhere between the purely peaceful and clearly violent. Obstructing access to airport terminals or blocking highways, for instance, needn't involve violence, but such tactics can all too easily be reframed in ways that can turn public attitudes against them. This in turn could help legitimise legal sanctions against protesters.

Because disruptive methods are ambiguous and vulnerable to political manipulation, difficult questions are never far away—and one of the thorniest is the question of what the word "violence" actually refers to.

Many political thinkers have argued over the respective merits of narrow definitions (where "violence" is chiefly seen as physical attack) and wider ones (encompassing indirect, unintended harm). Given that today's conscientious protesters face the risk that disruptive but nonviolent methods might be recategorised as violent security threats or their equivalent, a clear, narrow definition of violence is probably the safest for their purposes.

But there's another question to answer: even if violence is defined as the intentional infliction of physical harm against people or property, is it always absolutely unacceptable for protesters to commit acts of violence?

The Fine Line

For current protester leaders to encourage violence would be both morally unjustified and a serious tactical mistake. The outcome of any struggle between them and the government will be decided in large part by public opinion: if protesters can be blamed for starting violence, that will elevate the administration and its supporters. And worse yet, it might also help legitimise harsher methods by the security forces in response.

Some revolutionaries believe that there are times when violence is warranted, even against an authoritative force such as police or military.

But it's also a mistake to overstate the case against violence. For one thing, the claim that violence is never permissible under any circumstances probably isn't true—at least not if you're committed to the sort of liberal, republican, and democratic ideas that the US's founding fathers believed in.

Modern democratic thought has long held that individuals have a right to resist and rebel against tyrannical government and political injustices, and that defeating these great social evils may sometimes demand the resort to armed force. Properly understood, these sorts of ethics are highly restrictive: it's probably not justifiable for opponents of injustice to instigate violence. But if the defenders of an unjust government take the initiative, using violence as a means of deterring protest, that is a different matter.

As the English-American revolutionary Thomas Paine wrote in his 1776 pamphlet *Common Sense*, when struggling to defend rights against tyranny, "it is the violence which is done and threatened to our persons ... which conscientiously qualifies the use of arms."

This view of armed resistance still finds plenty of support across the spectrum of the US's political culture, though it's more frequently

cited on the political right than on the left. And its roots date back right to the start of the American project.

The right to resist tyranny and grave injustice was well understood by the 18th-century American revolutionaries, who drew inspiration from John Locke's *Second Treatise of Government,* published in 1689. Locke argued that if rulers exceeded their constitutional authority, the people would in principle be justified if they resorted to armed revolt. And when he drafted the American Declaration of Independence, Thomas Jefferson treated this idea as "self-evident."

And then there's the US Constitution's Second Amendment. Nowadays, the "right to keep and bear arms" that the amendment enshrines is most often defended by right-wingers, but it originated in 18th-century debates about the danger to the republic posed by permitting the state to monopolise the means of violence through the creation of a standing army. Proponents of the right to bear arms believed that a citizen militia would be a better bulwark against both foreign enemies and would-be tyrants within.

Another view widely accepted in the US (especially among advocates of gun ownership) is that innocent victims of violent attacks have a right to defend themselves. Nowadays, this right is more often discussed in cases of home invasion or other types of crime. But as Paine thought, the right to self-defence must also apply to those peacefully resisting injustice: if they are threatened with wrongful violence, then they too have a moral right to self-defence.

These core American beliefs all point to the same commitment: that civic resistance is sometimes justified, and that those who oppose injustice and tyranny are sometimes permitted violence in self-defence. To be clear, this isn't the same as suggesting that protesters ought to resort to arms. But if the left too eagerly rejects the idea that armed resistance can ever be justified, its leaders and footsoldiers will be vulnerable on two fronts.

Own Goals

First, it's naive to imagine that protest leaders are always in total control. Violence sometimes happens whether they sanction it or not.

This was the argument Nelson Mandela made to justify the ANC's use of sabotage: given the intensity of popular anger and outrage in South Africa, he said, the question wasn't whether violence would occur, but how to limit and guide it. The US certainly isn't at that point yet, but at least some outbreaks of violence are inevitable, and they might get worse over time.

Second, when violence does occur, those who are most hostile to the protesters will inevitably describe it as a self-evident wrong, morally as well as legally. An indiscriminate rejection of popular violence by protest leaders will be matched by that of the security forces.

The political scientist Erica Chenoweth rightly argues that any violent outbreaks now could seriously undercut the moral case Trump's opponents are trying to make. But if advocates of civil resistance stick to the line that "justified violence" is a contradiction in terms, they will simply hand the other side an argument to be used against them.

If violence seems likely for whatever reason, the opposition needs to be able to defend its members against any misrepresentation of their intentions. Refusing to acknowledge even hypothetical justifications for violence gives up on a vital line of defence.

EVALUATING THE AUTHOR'S ARGUMENTS:

Does viewpoint author Christopher J. Finlay's comparison between the justification of violence today and during the American Revolution hold water? Why or why not? Can you think of a comparison that would be more effective?

All Violent Rhetoric Should Be Condemned

Brian Harper

"*One byproduct of this factionalism is a hypocrisy which allows supporters to justify in their bloc what they condemn in another.*"

In the following viewpoint Brian Harper argues that today's partisan political climate has obscured reason. The author addresses reactions of members of the religious community to Donald Trump as his rhetoric and policies relate to Christian principles. He is particularly critical of those religious leaders who fail to rein in Trump because they are hopeful his administration will work to rid the Supreme Court of pro-choice justices. Harper is a public service fellow in Fordham University's International Political Economy and Development program.

AS YOU READ, CONSIDER THE FOLLOWING QUESTIONS:

1. Do US students respond with equal aversion to violent rhetoric on both sides of the political spectrum?
2. According to the viewpoint, how should religious ideals influence the strong social and political battles being waged in the US?
3. What current issues does this viewpoint bring up as proof that Catholics should not and do not always take right-wing stands?

"Not All Violent Rhetoric Is Condemned Equally," by Brian Harper, The National Catholic Reporter Publishing Company, July 20, 2017. Reprinted with permission of National Catholic Reporter Publishing Company, Kansas City, MO. NCRonline.org.

To say we live in an age of intense partisanship is about as obvious as acknowledging precipitation during a hailstorm.

"If you go back to the days of the Civil War, one can find cases in American political history where there was far more rancor and violence," said Stanford political scientist Shanto Iyengar. "But in the modern era, there are no 'ifs' and 'buts'—partisan animus is at an all-time high."

One byproduct of this factionalism is a special hypocrisy which allows hard-core supporters to justify in their bloc what they condemn in another. Look at the about-face both liberals and conservatives engaged in when Kathy Griffin held a likeness of President Donald Trump's decapitated head versus when Ted Nugent told President Barack Obama to "suck on my machine gun." Anyone who was disgusted by only one of these incidents might consider how deep their criteria for appropriate behavior truly run and whether they are part of our partisan problem.

Despite the duplicity, I suspect there are many Americans across the political spectrum who want all politicians to be held to the same standard, regardless of the letter that follows their name. As former Republican Rep. Bob Inglis Tweeted at Speaker of the House Paul Ryan, "You know that you would be inquiring into impeachment if this were a D."

In other words, the same yardstick ought to be used for everyone. If it was wrong for President Obama to do it, it should be wrong for President Trump as well.

What role might Christians play in putting this ideal into practice? Pope Francis said, "A good Catholic meddles in politics," while also urging believers to avoid the temptation of becoming "Christians of the 'right' or the 'left.'" The question, then, should not be what would a good Democrat or Republican do, but what would a good Christian do? What would Jesus do?

Refreshingly, many leaders in the US church seem to be taking this message to heart, calling out President Trump's policies that conflict with Catholic social teaching with vigor rivaling that which they demonstrated in challenging President Obama.

Some voices, however, have been noticeably quiet.

Bishop Robert Barron is one of the most prominent Catholic figures in the United States, with more than a million followers on

Some Americans are so beholden to their side or affiliation that they fail to reason.

Facebook. His Catholicism documentary series has become ubiquitous in confirmation and RCIA classes, and his Word on Fire online ministry provides insightful Catholic commentary on films, books, and news of the day.

Occasionally, Barron delves into politics. He reviewed President Obama's *The Audacity of Hope*, offering both praise for Obama's soaring rhetoric and criticism for his perceived discomfort in applying moral absolutes to politics and his pro-choice views, which Barron also found fault with in Sen. Edward Kennedy. In a video on Paul Ryan's claim that Catholic social teaching informs his economic vision, Barron deemed Ryan's explanation of the relationship between subsidiarity and solidarity as accurate. Intriguingly, he dismissed "a sort of Ayn Rand objectivism, whereby it's simply the pursuit of the individual self-interest that is given moral weight," as a threat to solidarity without contending with Ryan's well-known affinity for Rand.

Barron has had next to nothing to say about President Trump, but he recently waded into the Kathy Griffin controversy. After calling Griffin's photo what it was—"reprehensible"—he tried to place it in the broader context of a theme he often returns to: the breakdown of reasoned argument in American public life. From his perspective, the barbarity behind Griffin's image is part of this larger issue, which, he insisted, is evident in college protests throughout the United States.

"The American campus has become a place of violence," asserted Barron. "Conservative speakers ... are regularly bullied, and shouted down, and attacked, and, in some cases, really physically assaulted." The cause, he suggested, is "the almost complete lack of what we would classically call argument.

"I think there's a tight correlation between this kind of violence and the radical subjectivization of truth and ethical values that's been happening on the left now for a long time ... the complete relativizing of any claim to objective truth in the epistemological order or the moral order and instead the hyper-valorization of the self-creating will."

Barron diagnosed this as "voluntarism," or "the valorization of voluntas, will, over intellectus, over mind. The will has primacy. The will to power has primacy over any claim to truth." The solution he presented is a "much better epistemology, that is to say, a much clearer account of objective truth."

Barron was right to identify a collapse in rational debate in our country, though he failed to distinguish between people who have reached a different conclusion than he has about the truth of a particular matter and those who do not believe in the existence of objective truth at all. Someone who disagrees with him that same-sex marriage is morally problematic, for example, does not necessarily think there is no such thing as absolute truth; they might simply believe his conviction on that matter is wrong.

He also grossly overstated the violence he sees in college students who protest conservative speakers. At the very least, he did not concede that reacting to people with whom one disagrees using aggression rather than logic is not unique to "the left," as evinced by Rep.

Greg Gianforte and a number of Trump rallies.

All this brings us to the elephant in the room, or rather, the White House. To single out college students, Kathy Griffin, and "the left" as culprits in the disintegration of valid debate or trust in moral absolutes is an extraordinarily selective reading of the problem.

President Trump, to quote his predecessor, is "not really a facts guy." While the president's dishonesty sometimes looks like a calculated tool to get what he wants (which, in his defense, is not exactly new in politics), in many cases, he genuinely seems to believe in the power of the "self-creating will" with which Barron took such issue. The truth in his eyes is apparently whatever he thinks it is at a given moment, despite any evidence to the contrary. When asked by a lawyer if he had lied about how much money he has, he responded, "My net worth fluctuates, and it goes up and down with markets and with attitudes and with feelings, even my own feelings, but I try."

This faith in one's ability to determine what is and is not real extends throughout the president's administration, with advisor Kellyanne Conway famously defending press secretary Sean Spicer's lies about the size of President Trump's inauguration crowd as "alternative facts."

It is unreasonable to expect Barron to perfectly balance his analysis of every issue to prove his lack of bias. Not every example can be cited to make a point, and with President Trump's mendacity well documented, one could argue that there is no need for Barron to add fuel to the fire. Given his considerate and consistent objections to liberal politicians, however, Barron's unwillingness to speak out when President Trump and other Republicans fall short of Catholicism's standards is unsettling.

There is a perception that the hierarchy of the American Catholic Church is in lockstep with the Republican Party. It is important to note that this view is not exclusively held by liberals, atheists, or people who are averse to the faith. I have seen many devout Catholics express their dismay at bishops and priests who, in the run-up to the 2016 election, informed their flock that when they went to the polls, their sole concern should be choosing a candidate who opposes abortion. Never mind any proposed Muslim ban. Never mind climate change denial, which flies in the face of priorities Pope Francis has raised as absolutely essential for Catholics. Never mind promises to repeal legislation which has expanded health care coverage for millions with "something terrific." The "terrific" bills being considered could leave more than 20 million people without insurance.

These concerned Catholics were not expecting bishops or priests to endorse Hillary Clinton or disregard the church's defense of life. They simply wondered if there were any political sins that would not be instantly absolved by opposition to abortion.

To be fair, the United States Conference of Catholic Bishops has risen to the occasion since the inauguration. They recently said that elements of the Senate's Better Care Reconciliation Act would "wreak havoc on low-income families and struggling communities and must not be supported." The bishops praised the U.S. Court of Appeals for the 9th Circuit's decision upholding the preliminary injunction on President Trump's travel ban, and they called his withdrawal from the Paris Climate Agreement "deeply troubling." As Jesuit Fr. Thomas Reese, said, "Some bishops argue that they have spoken out on these other issues but that the media only covers the bishops when they participate in the culture wars."

That is why Barron's silence is so regrettable. In overlooking President Trump's culpability in violent rhetoric and "radical subjectivization"—both of which clearly upset him—Barron is playing into the partisan narrative that certain sins are worse when certain people commit them, that a D-List celebrity's brutality is worse than the president's.

Ironically, he gives the impression that the call to objective moral truth should be subjectively applied.

Viewpoint author Brian Harper writes about hypocrisy among religious leaders and the need for them to address such issues about which young people feel strongly, such as climate change and universal health care. How does this apply to student protest?

Violent Protests Can Bring About Positive Change

Marco Palma

> "We have to realize violent protests can be just as efficient and well organized as non-violent ones."

In the following viewpoint Marco Palma cites the most disturbing events in world history to argue that violence can create positive change. He believes that such catastrophes as slavery, the Holocaust, apartheid, the rape of Nanking, and the subjugation of Native Americans all called for violent self-defense and overthrow of power. The author cites Black Lives Matter as an example of a group that could justify violence as the only way to get voices heard and force action. Palma further contends that the media's negativity toward the justification of violence has resulted in nonviolence being embraced as the only acceptable form of protest. Palma is a staff writer for *The Narrator*.

"Violent Protests Are an Effective Tool to Achieve Social Change," by Marco Palma, December 12, 2016. Reprinted by permission. The Narrator is a non-conformist publishing platform that helps others tell their story in order that all may have greater understanding of the human experience. https://narratorjournal.com.

1. Can violence be justified by those who believe strongly on one side of an issue if they understand that the other side can be justified to use it as well?
2. Does the desire to draw attention to an issue justify the use of violence?
3. How does the author frame the media in a negative light as it relates to recent well-publicized protests?

I write this article in defense of Black Lives Matter and in defense of Flag Burning. Violent protests are very effective in drawing needed attention towards evident issues in society that require immediate change. There are many situations across the country and even around the world that would have never made newspaper headlines or gathered anyone's curiosity if not for the violent behavior of those protesting. I am going to discuss which pressures influence people to react boldly to the problems that affect their daily lives. In order to help those watching current events unfold, understand that these protestors are people, just like them, that have good reason to react the way they do. It is necessary to find out why people feel that violence is the most effective way to make their voices heard; perhaps they are not receiving any help from their state or federal government. There are instances where violent protests do in fact achieve results; aggressive protests can be just as effective as non-violent ones. Nonviolence sometimes produces no change nor gains any momentum, so we should not blame violent protestors for doing what they believe to be effective, as circumstances are different in every situation.

The way our news channels and online media frames these outbursts really does affect the way we view these moments and the individuals who do decide to act out by violently protesting for their rights. Usually the motives behind violent protests are either to subjugate, persuade or intimidate the audience. Recent cases like the election of Donald Trump, groups have been attempting to persuade us to believe that what they are fighting for is justified, and that everyone deserves to live without the fear of being harmed by the police, other citizens, and their own governments. We all deserve to have our voices heard when we feel that our current situation is unfair or unjust, however when the media portrays groups as hostile or out of line, we tend to believe the news channel. We are not provided with any statistical information or potential reason as to how things became so intolerable. We are only given images and videos of people running around destroying public property. The way the internet, news channels, and other forms of social media present information to us does affect how we view the people who decide to fight for their rights and how we think about the necessary violence that is occurring.

Like the people of Ferguson, Missouri, many individuals in this tense political climate felt trapped within their particular circumstances. They knew that protesting was their only option. They are not to blame for the lack of proper representation which could have prevented all of the unrest. Over the last year and a half, I have seen many riots, protests, and social revolutions appear in countries like Venezuela, Mexico and Germany, as well as in my own communities. I admit that I have walked with and have pushed with them in protest. These protesters do not carry the same ideas about violence that we do, in most cases, especially in Mexico [where] the people know that violence is the only thing that will make their voices heard. We have to realize it does take a lot of harm and injustice to make individuals picket or protest. What I will be exploring is what is happening to these people, what issues make them restless enough to take action.

There are many cases around the world where violence is the only appropriate response to oppression for example. In Mexico, the federal government has taken a laissez-faire approach to the drug cartels that run rampant across the country. Since the government has no idea of how to deal with the problem, innocent men and women are being harmed. Instead of simply waiting to be kidnapped or killed by members of drug cartels, the population decided to take to the street and put pressure on the government and the groups that are harming the country.

Dr. Robert Meadow, a PhD professor at the University of Southern California, takes on the issue by holding that not all acts of violence fall under the same umbrella. Dr. Meadow splits up the

Rioters took to the streets after a black teen was killed by a white police officer in Missouri. The riots succeeded in bringing the issue of racial relations to the forefront.

acts into three different categories: domestic violence, criminal violence and interpersonal violence. He states that most violence occurs in private he infers that while most of the violence we witness is on the news that the larger incidents of violence in fact occur in private. We have to understand that the media usually never covers the consistent acts of private violence. The only time we even see "private acts of violence" is when "they are occasionally recorded by means of cell phone, home video, cameras, and nanny cams". The only time these videos as broadcasted to the public are when they, almost accidentally, spread too quickly to be suppressed before they go viral. In other words when videos go viral they do not expose the isolated incidents of violence that are occurring in a neighborhood they are in fact exposing the day to day realities of that [community]. The only time the media, and ultimately our society as a whole, believes that using excessive force is necessary is when we have to use police action or military force to harm others in order to protect us. Like Meadow, Taylor Adams, a senior news editor for the *New York Times*, believes that the media does not portray violent outbursts in the appropriate light. He writes about the violent outburst that occurred after the grand jury of New York City decided not to indict police officer Daniel Pantaleo for the death of fellow New Yorker Eric Garner. He suggests that covering the protesting as wrong and inhumane ignores the issue that many internal social pressures caused ordinary people to believe that nonviolence would not help them. A quote he uses to sum up the actions taken by the protestors is, "we revolt simply because, for many reasons, we can no longer breathe" and I believe this does help justify why they cause public damage. These protestors are simply trying to get effective news coverage even Adams realized that in a separate case in Ferguson, Missouri "if protestors hadn't looted and burnt down that QuikTrip on the second day, Ferguson would not be a point of worldwide attention".

The type of violence that I am discussing does not limit itself to the picket line or can be summed up to simple looting. Aggressively attacking the media and putting constant pressure on your political representatives in order to help keep your best interest in mind is also a form of violent protesting. Violence is what draws people's attention to any movement and what will hopefully happen is the acknowledgment of the real issue. Any publicity towards your purpose is always good publicity. Getting the media on your side is key to spreading the idea you want. In the case of Ferguson, Missouri, the idea was the suffocation of a whole community under the largely white police department. In many cases the issues can range from the acknowledgement of global warming to getting equal pay for farm workers, we have to realize violent protests can be just as efficient and well organized as non-violent ones.

Kimberly Brownlee a senior lecturer at the University of Manchester, would agree with Adams, and Meadow's idea that the media unfairly treats protesters like criminals and that these individuals are well within their rights to protect themselves from unfair treatment by their society. She states that "in democratic societies, civil disobedience as such is not a crime" when protesters engage in civil disobedience they should not be punished for the action of protesting but only for the damage that they cause. The media tends to overlook the reasons and justifications citizens have to protest and instead attempt to distract us with the violence within a revolt. However, what she does make clear is that while yes protesting is legal and violent protesting is well within our rights, if we destroy property or break the law we are responsible for the damage that we do cause. She further explains that "like non-violence, a willingness to accept the legal consequences normally is preferable and often has a positive impact on the disobedient cause". We should remember that when people come together and riot, like in the case in Eric Garner and Daniel Pantaleo of the State of New York they do it because "Peaceful Protesting is a luxury for those who can be assured that their voices will be heard without violence" (Adams). There is no guarantee that the protestors will bring an end to the social pressures that cause them to revolt but they are well within their rights to bring attention to harmful policies even if that involves looting or burning down a quick trip gas station. We cannot allow the amount of destruction caused by such movements to take our attention away from the real cause of what people are fighting for.

So far it has been very clear which form of violence I have been talking about but in a time when we can be violent without having to cause anyone any harm. Cesar Chavez is one character in history that fought for the rights of many farm workers across the country and while he began his campaign as strictly nonviolent he soon understood that the only way to succeed was by keeping the media on his side. He knew that if he had enough undeniable evidence that the food growers were treating their day laborers inhumanly, the food distributing companies had to give in to his demands. This is an entirely different form of violence; Cesar Chavez had developed a way to be passive aggressive yet still harsh. No matter how subtle his methods appeared to be he was still violently attacking whoever was in his way. Through boycotting company products, slandering a company's name in the press or video and collecting massive amounts of evidence that could not be denied in court. Cesar Chavez managed to attack many companies without causing any physical harm, while causing just as much damage.

It's a mistake to believe that democracy goes hand and hand with peaceful protesting. Violent civil disobedience does not only occur in America and the causes that bring these situations to the forefront of the public eye are not

unique to North America or the United States. Protestors decide to become violent for the same reasons, even if they begin strictly nonviolent. Elizabeth Barber, a writer and editor for *Time* magazine, writes about a peaceful group of student protestors in Hong Kong that in December of 2012 decided to turn violent after two months of peaceful marching and protesting. These students are fighting for a Pro-Democracy government and were requesting the ability of free elections. After about two months of being ignored by the government and harassed by local officials, the students decided that they needed a new way to make their voices heard. As one of the bystanders reported says "I think we have had enough, I'm ready to fight ready to protect our people, ready for revolution". Things began getting out of hand when local police officers decided to start beating on protesters and anyone that stood in their way, later the students were arrested and the police department denied any form of maltreatment. We can clearly see why these students were so displeased with their government, first they're ignored and then beaten for peacefully standing up for what they believe to be correct. Yes, the students decided to fight back but what is ignored is "police also hackled protesters, tearing down their banners calling for real democracy, and at times it became unclear who [was] aggressing whom".

There are situations where it's obvious that the national Government is ignoring a very abrupt issue, take for example the kidnapping of 43 students in Mexico a year ago. There is a similar case to Barber's article written by Loan Grillo, a senior correspondent for the GlobalPost. In late 2014 the kidnapping of 43 students from Iguala, Mexico finally forced the Mexican government to face the issue of drug violence that has taken over the large part of their society. Many Mexican citizens have decided to come together and create a hostile environment for the drug cartels that have been taking complete advantage of the people and of their national government. There has been violent outburst all over Mexico to protest the lack of support the president Enrique Peña Nieto and government has given them. We have to understand that "in the end, it took a crime that was shocking even by the standards of Mexico's blood soaked drug war for a semblance of order to return" this is what caused all of these citizens to finally come together and fight back. People become violent when they realize that the authorities are not going to help keep them safe or stand up for their rights. In Iguala, Mexico many police officers were actually working with the local drug dealers and people [became] so afraid that they just stopped asking the police department for help "we would hear gunshots, sometimes we would hear screams. Of course I never called the police. The police were with the murderers".

Violent outbursts have been the only effective method of achieving any form of social order throughout the United States of America and the united states of Mexico. People decide to become violent when public officials turn a blind eye to all of the problems that threaten their society. Alan Chin, a contributing photographer for the *New York Times* and the Chinese magazine *Modern Weekly*, [points out] that democracy is mistakenly seen to go hand and hand with peaceful protesting. People decide to use violence as a form of protests when they see no other option available. Chin makes it clear "that people only feel compelled to protest if they are outraged enough," he talks about the city of Ferguson, Missouri and its citizens reactions to the death of a young black teenager. There must already have been an issue with the way police officers were treating the people within this community if they believed that causing physical harm was [their] only viable option. We have to understand that people decide to become violent because "real damage sends signals to all sides that the problem is serious and critical".

EVALUATING THE AUTHOR'S ARGUMENTS:

Does viewpoint author Marco Palma's use of historical horrors as examples convince you that violence is sometimes the answer? How did he convince you or fail to convince you? Could you use other historical examples to argue that the opposite is true? What examples would you use?

Don't Let Street Violence Distract from the Message

Robert Levering

In the following viewpoint Robert Levering argues that creative protest can send a message more effectively than violent street tactics ever could. The author shares his experience as an antiwar activist during the Vietnam War and the important steps he and fellow organizers took to ensure their message of peace was not disrupted by radical terrorist group the Weather Underground. The government, he explains, actually prefers violent protest because it can use such actions to provoke fear among the people and advance their own agenda. Levering worked as full-time anti-Vietnam war organizer with such groups as AFSC and the New Mobilization Committee and Peoples Coalition for Peace and Justice.

AS YOU READ, CONSIDER THE FOLLOWING QUESTIONS:
1. What are Black Bloc tactics according to the viewpoint?
2. Why do the Weathermen's actions during the Days of Rage serve as a good case study according to the author?
3. What purpose did the marshals serve during the demonstration?

O nly the Vietnam era protests match the size and breadth of the movement unleashed by the election of Donald Trump. One point of comparison: The massive march and rally against the Vietnam War in 1969 was the largest political demonstration in American history until the even more massive Women's March in January.

All around us we can see signs that the movement has only just begun. Consider, for instance, that a large percentage of those in the Women's March engaged in their very first street protest. Or that thousands of protesters spontaneously flocked to airports to challenge the anti-Muslim ban. Or that hundreds of citizens have confronted their local congressional representatives at their offices and town hall meetings about the potential repeal of Obamacare and other Trump/ Republican policies.

As activists prepare for future demonstrations, many are rightfully concerned about the potential disruptions by those using Black Bloc tactics, which involve engaging in property destruction and physical attacks on police and others. They often appear at demonstrations dressed in black and cover their faces to disguise their identities. Their numbers have been relatively small to date. But they garner an outsized amount of media coverage, such as a violent protest in Berkeley to block an appearance by an alt-right provocateur or the punching of a white nationalist during Trump's inauguration. The result is that an otherwise peaceful demonstration's primary message can get lost in a fog of rock throwing and tear gas. Even worse, fewer people are likely to turn up at future protests, and potential allies get turned off.

This is not a new phenomenon. Gandhi and Martin Luther King, Jr. confronted this issue. So did those of us active in the struggle against the Vietnam War. I played a major role in organizing the national antiwar demonstrations between 1967 and 1971, as well as

Violent protests often do a disservice to the protesters' cause and bolster the opposite side. The author believes that peaceful protest is much more effective.

dozens of smaller actions during that time. Today's protest organizers and participants can learn much from our experiences on the frontlines a half century ago.

A good place to start is to consider the Weathermen, the most prominent of the counterparts to the Black Bloc in our day. As proponents of violent street tactics, the Weathermen capitalized on an aspect of the '60s counterculture that glorified violent revolution. Posters displaying romanticized images of Che Guevara, Viet Cong soldiers (especially women fighters) and Black Panthers with guns were plastered on many walls.

The Weathermen didn't just spout revolutionary rhetoric. One of their most memorable actions was what they proclaimed as the "Days of Rage." They urged people to join them in Chicago in early October 1969 to "Bring the War Home." They recruited extensively among white working-class youths to come to the city with helmets and such weapons as clubs, prepared to vandalize businesses and cars as well as assault police. They believed their action would help provoke an uprising against the capitalist state.

During the "Days of Rage," the Weathermen did not attach themselves to a larger peaceful demonstration. They were on their own. So, the action provides a great case study about the feasibility of violent street tactics.

For starters, they discovered that it was hard to find recruits for their violent street army. Only about 300 people showed up despite months of effort. And they found it harder to enlist support for their actions even among those who were friendly with them politically. In fact, Fred Hampton, the leader of the Black Panther Party in Chicago, publicly denounced the group's action, fearing it would turn off potential allies and lead to intensified police repression. "We believe that the Weathermen action is anarchistic, opportunistic, individualistic, chauvinistic and Custeristic [referring to General George Custer's suicidal Last Stand]. It's child's play. It's folly."

It would not be overstating the case to say that the "Days of Rage" was a flop. They did trash some stores and engage in fights with police. But Chicago police easily contained their violence and rounded up virtually all of the militants and charged them with stiff crimes. Some suffered serious injuries, and several were shot by police (none fatally). The Weathermen soon gave up on violent street protests, became the Weather Underground and confined themselves to symbolic bombings of such targets as police stations and a bathroom in the US Capitol.

In short, the "Days of Rage" shows the ineffectiveness of violent street tactics unless combined with a larger peaceful protest. The Black Bloc anarchists understand this reality, too. They need us as a cover for their actions. Put another way: We don't need them, but they need us. So, the primary way to deal with those who advocate violent tactics is to isolate them, do everything possible to separate them from the peaceful demonstration. That was one of our goals in 1969 when organizing the November 15 antiwar march on Washington, DC.

As organizers, we knew that it was not enough to stop potential disrupters. We knew we had to make sure that the demonstration itself would channel people's indignation with the war more creatively than yet another conventional march and rally. People take to the streets because they are upset, angry or disillusioned. They want to express their outrage as powerfully as possible. Although some people prefer disruption for its own sake, almost everyone else wants to deliver their message so that it leads to positive social change, not make matters worse.

We adopted a tactic first used by a group of Quakers the previous summer. To personalize the war's impact, that group read the names of the American soldiers killed in Vietnam from the steps of the Capitol. Their weekly civil disobedience action received a lot of media attention, particularly after some members of Congress joined them. Before long, peace groups throughout the land were reading the names of the war dead in their town squares and other public spaces.

For our demonstration in Washington, we planned what we called the "March Against Death." Here is how *Time* magazine described it at the time: "Disciplined in organization, friendly in mood, [the march] started at Arlington National Cemetery, went past the front of the White House and on to the west side of the Capitol. Walking single file and grouped by states, the protesters carried devotional candles and 24-in. by 8-in. cardboard signs, each bearing the name of a man killed in action or a Vietnamese village destroyed by the war. The candles flickering in the wind, the funereal rolling of drums, the hush over most of the line of march—but above all, the endless recitation of names of dead servicemen and gutted villages as each marcher passed the White House—were impressive drama."

First in line was the widow of a fallen serviceman, followed by 45,000 marchers (the number of Americans killed in the war to that date). After walking the four-mile route, the marchers reached the Capitol, where they placed their placards in coffins. The march began the evening of November 13 and went on for 36 hours. No one who was there would ever forget. It also set the tone for the massive march and rally.

While the "March Against Death" was taking place, we were busily training marshals who would oversee the demonstration—that is, essentially be our own force of nonviolent peacekeepers. We were rightfully concerned that groups of Weathermen-style protesters would disrupt our demonstration regardless of how creative our tactics were. The Chicago action had taken place only a month earlier, and we knew that there were many individuals and small groups for whom the appeal of violent street tactics had not diminished.

With the help of several churches that provided us with spaces, we recruited trainers, many with previous experience in nonviolent training. After giving an overview of the march's objectives and logistics, we had the trainees do several role-playing exercises. For instance, we had a scenario where a group of Weathermen-style protesters tried to disrupt the march by trying to get people to join them in more "militant" actions. One tactic we suggested was to get the marchers to sing the then-popular John Lennon tune "Give Peace a Chance" to divert attention from the disrupters. Another was to get the marshals to link their arms to separate the disrupters from the rest of the marchers.

At the end of the two-hour-long session, the newly trained marshals were given a white armband and told where to meet the next day. We trained more than 4,000 marshals who were deployed along the entire route of the march. The armbands were an important symbol to help us isolate would-be disrupters.

Although there were a few incidents after the rally had broken up, they did not detract from the powerful message that the half-million war opponents in Washington conveyed to the public and the nation's leaders. The war didn't end the next day, or even the next year, but the peace movement played a major role in stopping it—something that was unprecedented in American history.

Not everyone was pleased with our marshals. In Clara Bingham's interview of Weathermen leader Bill Ayers for her recently published book, *Witness to the Revolution*, Ayers said: " … the problem with the mass mobilizations at that time was that the militants—us— were always contained. We were pushed aside by peace marshals and demonstration marshals."

The man in the White House also did not like the peaceful character of our actions. In *Nixonland*, historian Rick Perlstein tells a story that indicates what kind of protest Richard Nixon would have preferred: "A briefing paper came to the president's desk in the middle of March [1969] instructing him to expect increased violence on college campuses that spring. 'Good!' he wrote across the face."

This anecdote points out another significant lesson from the Vietnam era. Governments invariably welcome violent protests. With soldiers, police and huge arsenals of weapons, they know how to deal with any form of violence. They also infiltrate protest groups with provocateurs to stir up violence—something we experienced repeatedly then and is certainly happening today. The Black Bloc is especially vulnerable to infiltration because of their anonymity. And, as we learned then, those in power will willfully mischaracterize peaceful demonstrators as violent to help turn those in the middle against us.

What makes any resort to violence, including property destruction, on the part of the movement especially dangerous today is the current occupant of the White House. Most of us have seen video clips of the campaign rally last year where Trump said he would like to see a heckler "carried out on a stretcher."

We can only imagine what this man would do if given any excuse to fully deploy the forces of violent repression against us. Nor can we forget that this man has shown a willingness, if not eagerness, to encourage his gun-toting supporters to turn on his opponents.

The movement must keep its focus on the issues. We must not allow ourselves to get distracted. Too many lives are threatened by Trump's reckless rhetoric and heartless policies. We can succeed, just as we did in stopping the Vietnam War. It will take time, but we can create a more just and peaceful society. It starts with us.

EVALUATING THE AUTHOR'S ARGUMENTS:

Viewpoint author Robert Levering uses his experience from the Vietnam War era to advise today's protestors. Do you think the tactics of those organizers can be applied to the unrest in the United States today? Why or why not?

Facts About School Protests

Editor's note: These facts can be used in reports to add credibility when making important points or claims.

- The first organized student protesters in the United States joined the Student Nonviolent Coordinating Committee, which was basically the student group of the civil rights movement of the early 1960s.
- Many students joined the Freedom Riders. Some were beaten by racist southerners as they actively worked for integration.
- Among the issues embraced by student civil rights workers was voting rights. African Americans could not vote in the south before the Voting Rights Act of 1965.
- Some African American students participated in lunch counter sit-ns in the early 1960s. Many were arrested as they tried to integrate lunch counters.
- What became known as the Greensboro Four were African American college students that sat at a lunch counter in North Carolina and refused to budge until they were served. Their arrests sparked others to take similar action.
- About 300 young people joined the Greensboro Four in early 1960. The lunch counter sit-ins soon expanded to 50 cities. They were soon to be integrated.
- Student activism in the early-to-mid 1960s called attention to segregation and discrimination in the South. The participating students helped bring about integration and freedom for African Americans.
- The seeds of the free speech movement in the United States were planted by students at Berkeley led by fiery speaker Mario Savio. Berkeley became a hotbed of student protest in the 1960s.
- One sit-in at Berkeley that protested administration policies at the school resulted in about 800 arrests.

- The *Tinker v. Des Moines* case that reached the Supreme Court in 1969 resulted in a ruling that students have the right to free expression if the learning process at schools is not disrupted.
- The deadliest campus protest of the Vietnam War era occurred at Kent State University in Ohio. It was there that four students were killed by National Guardsmen on May 4, 1970.
- Protests against the Vietnam War in 1970 were not limited to Kent State. The shootings there, however, resulted in campus uprisings throughout the country that resulted in many schools shutting down.
- Among the schools that experienced tragedy in 1970 was at Jackson State, a black college in Mississippi. Two students were killed there by area police during an antiwar protest.
- Not all student activism has targeted issues in the United States. Students organized sit-ins and other activities in the 1970s and 1980s to protest racial apartheid in South Africa. Their work helped topple apartheid in 1981.
- Thousands of courageous high school students in Soweto, South Africa, protested apartheid policies that limited educational opportunities in June 1976. They were met by police that eventually opened fire, killing two and injuring hundreds.
- The Soweto shootings sparked massive black protests in Soweto, resulting in the use of armored tanks to restore order. The events in Soweto played a major role in the ending of apartheid five years later.
- One of the bravest student uprisings against oppression occurred at Tiananmen Square in Beijing, China, in 1989. Tanks killed thousands while police arrested an estimated 10,000.
- Perhaps the boldest protest in world history was conducted by a student group known as the White Rose society during the Nazi period in Germany. Siblings Sophie Scholl and Hans Scholl secretly distributed anti-government material during World War II.
- Hans and Sophie Scholl were caught distributing anti-government leaflets at the University of Munich in 1943. They and other White Rose leaders were convicted by a trump court and

executed, but they became and remain heroes in post-Nazi Germany.

- So entrenched was Nazi propaganda during World War II that the White Rose participants were condemned by most University of Munich students during a pro-government rally.
- The fall of Communism in Czechoslovakia was sparked by students that bravely conducted a march in November 1989. An attack by police resulted in 167 marchers being hospitalized.
- Eleven days after the student march in Czechoslovakia, which sparked massive strikes, the Communists relinquished power in that country. Students played a major role in the downfall of Communism throughout Eastern Europe.
- Pro-democracy student demonstrators in Hong Kong staged what became known as the Umbrella Protests in 2014. Joined by other citizens, the students used umbrellas to shield them from police tear gas and pepper spray.
- Student protests during the divisive year of 1968 were not only held in the United States. Students in France and Poland also staged protests against their governments that year.
- A series of small battles between Iranian students and police in 1999 led to officers raiding a dormitory at the University of Tehran. The action resulted in at least 20 wounded and 125 jailed.
- The repression of Iranian students in 1999 inspired a demonstration by more than 10,000 students from that country. Student activism has since remained strong in Iran.
- The Black Lives Matter movement that was launched in 2013 resulted in many protests against police shootings of unarmed African American men.
- The most contentious Black Lives Matter protest occurred in Ferguson, Missouri, in August 2014. The protests in that town after police had shot and killed unarmed black teenager Michael Brown grew violent.
- Ferguson was not the only place in Missouri in which protests occurred. Students at the University of Missouri protested after several racist incidents had occurred on the campus in 2015.

- The University of Missouri protests gained success when the school's football team threatened to strike and not play its next game. The result was the resignation of school president Tim Wolfe, which was considered a victory for the students.

Organizations to Contact

The editors have compiled the following list of organizations concerned with the issues debated in this book. The descriptions are derived from materials provided by the organizations. All have publications or information available for interested readers. The list was compiled on the date of publication of the present volume; the information provided here may change. Be aware that many organizations take several weeks or longer to respond to inquiries, so allow as much time as possible for the receipt of requested materials.

American Civil Liberties Union (ACLU)
125 Broad Street, 18th Floor, New York, NY 10004
phone: (212) 549–2500
email: aclupreferences@aclu.org
website: www.aclu.org
The American Civil Liberties Union uses its resources to fight for and preserve individual rights and freedoms in the United States.

Black Youth Project 100
PO Box 9031, Chicago, IL 60609
Phone: (773) 940–1800
email: info@byp100.org
website: www.byp.org
This organization works to empower African Americans politically while strengthening communities through organizing, fundraising and promoting public debate.

Campus Pride
PO Box 240473, Charlotte, NC 28224
phone: (704) 277–6710
email: info@campuspride.org
website: www.campuspride.org

Campus Pride is the only national nonprofit organization for student leaders and campus groups working to foster a safer college environment for LGBT students.

Center for American Progress
133 H Street NW, Washington, DC 20005
phone: (202) 682–1611
email: www.americanprogress.org/about/contact-us
website: www.americanprogress.org
Among the many missions of this organization is to help college students afford a quality education and maximize their educational experiences. The Center for American Progress seeks to move the country forward in a progressive direction.

Democracy Matters
201 Riverview Drive, Poughkeepsie, NY 12601-3935
Phone: (315) 725–4211
email: www.democracymatters.org/contact-democracy-matters
website: www.democracymatters.org
Democracy Matters helps students organize projects connecting pro-democracy reforms on such issues as the environment, civil rights, education, and health care. Its goal is to reduce the role of money and increase the role of activists into the American political system.

Hip Hop Congress
50 Woodside Road, #203, Redwood City, CA 94061
phone: (213) 215–5257
email: hiphopcongressinc@gmail.com
website: www.hiphopcongress.com
Hip Hop Congress is a network of individuals and organizations seeking to change the world by uplifting culture for the creative development of artists and young people. The organization works to achieve its goals through education, civic engagement, and equitable resource exchange.

Project Mobilize
7674 W. 63rd Street, Summit, IL 60501
email: www.mobilize.org/join-the-movement
website: www.mobilize.org
Project Mobilize is a network of leaders targeting millennials that seeks to create positive change within the system and through existing organizations. It also works to invest in new ideas that would help unify Americans in a progressive manner.

Young America's Foundation
11480 Commerce Park Drive, Suite 600, Reston, VA 20191-1556
phone: (703) 318–9608
email: https://www.yaf.org/contact-us/
website: www.yaf.org
This conservative student group seeks to increase the number of students that are motivated toward ideas of individual freedom, a strong national defense, free enterprise, and traditional values.

Young Democratic Socialists of America
705 Maiden Lane, Suite 702, New York, NY 10038
phone: (917) 830–8416
email: www.mobilize.org/join-the-movement
website: https://y.dsausa.org/contact-us/
This political organization works to build the power of students, campus communities, and youth to fight for equality, justice, and democratic socialism.

For Further Reading

Books

Sigal R. Ben-Porath, *Free Speech on Campus*. Philadelphia, PA: University of Pennsylvania Press, 2017.

The author of this book examines the current state of the arguments revolving around free speech on campus. She uses real-world examples to explore the contexts in which conflicts arise and also touches on issues of identity politics.

Richard Delgado and Jean Stefancic, *Must We Defend Nazis? Why the First Amendment Should Not Protect Hate Speech and White Supremacy*. New York, NY: NYU Press, 2018.

The authors of this book claim that hate speech on campuses and on the internet should not be afforded First Amendment protection. The book was updated after the contentious white nationalist rally in Charlottesville in 2017.

Roderick A. Ferguson, *We Demand: The University and Student Protests*. Oakland, CA: University of California Press, 2017.

This book serves as an education and a warning to Americans in its claim that their universities are becoming its institutions that eschew social advancements in favor of anti-intellectualism. The author believes that progressiveness is being widely attacked on campuses.

Mark Kurlansky, *1968: The Year that Rocked the World*. New York, NY: Random House, 2008.

This book details one of the most explosive years in American and world history. Among the events covered were what has been described as police riots against antiwar protesters during the Democratic National Convention in Chicago.

David S. Meyer, *The Politics of Protest: Social Movements in America*. Cary, NC: Oxford University Press, 2014.

A professor of sociology at the University of California, author David S. Meyer offers here a historical overview for understanding social movements and political protest in the United States. He also sets an analytic framework for such events.

John Palfrey, *Safe Spaces, Brave Spaces: Diversity and Free Expression in Education*. Cambridge, MA: The MIT Press, 2017.

Palfrey, a former Harvard University professor who serves as Head of School at Phillips Academy, offers here that values of diversity and free expression should coexist on campus. He adds that the two are more compatible than widely believed.

Nadine Strossen, *Hate: Why We Should Resist It with Free Speech, Not Censorship*. Cary, NC: Oxford University Press, 2018.

A professor of law at the New York Law School, Nadine Strossen argues in her book in favor of the First Amendment guarantees of freedom of speech and democracy. She believes they are compatible with the ideals of equality and the striving for societal harmony.

Keith E. Whittington, *Speak Freely: Why Universities Must Defend Free Speech*. Princeton, NJ: Princeton University Press, 2018.

The author of this book argues that schools must protect and encourage free speech, which he views as their lifeblood. Whittington expresses his view that without free speech, a university cannot fulfill its fundamental and necessary purpose to encourage freedom of thought, ideological diversity, and tolerance.

Periodicals and Internet Sources

Maggie Astor, "7 Times in History When Students Turned to Activism," *New York Times*, March 5, 2018. https://www.nytimes.com/2018/03/05/us/student-protest-movements.html

John Bacon and Christal Hayes, "'We Deserve Better': Students Nationwide Walk Out in Massive Protest Over Gun Violence," *USA Today*, March 15, 2018. https://www.usatoday.com/story/news/2018/03/14/thousands-students-across-u-s-walk-out-class-today-protest-gun-violence/420731002/

Aryn Baker, "This Photo Galvanized the World Against Apartheid. Here's the Story Behind It," *Time*, June 15, 2016. http://time.com/4365138/soweto-anniversary-photograph/

Macie J. Bartkowski, "From China to Poland, Lessons from June 4, 1989," Waging Nonviolence, June 3, 2014. https://wagingnonviolence.org/feature/lessons-polands-peaceful-transition-tiananmen-crackdown-25-years-later/

Arian Campo-Flores, "Gun-Violence Protests Draw an Estimated 1 Million Students," *Wall Street Journal*, March 15, 2018. https://www.wsj.com/articles/students-plan-national-school-walkout-to-protest-shootings-1521019801

Lyle Denniston, "The Campus and the Vietnam War: Protest and Tragedy," *Constitution Daily*, September 26, 2017. https://constitutioncenter.org/blog/the-campus-and-the-vietnam-war-protest-and-tragedy

Isabel Fattal, "What Will the Nationwide School Walkouts Accomplish?" *The Atlantic*, March 14, 2018. https://www.theatlantic.com/education/archive/2018/03/what-will-the-nationwide-walkouts-accomplish/555638/

Daniel J. Flynn, "Megaphone Mark and the Columbia Takeover 50 Years Later," *The American Spectator*, April 27, 2018. https://spectator.org/megaphone-mark-the-columbia-takeover-50-years-later/

Sarah Gray, "What to Know about March for Our Lives and Other Student-Led Gun Control Protests," *Time*, March 12, 2018. http://time.com/5165794/student-protests-walkouts-florida-school-shooting/

Holocaust Education and Archive Research Team. "The White Rose," Holocaust Research Project. http://www.holocaustresearchproject.org/revolt/whiterose.html

Ma Jian, "Tianenman Square 25 Years Later: 'Every Person in the Crowd was a Victim of the Massacre,'" *The Guardian*, June 1, 2014. https://www.theguardian.com/world/2014/jun/01/tiananmen-square-25-years-every-person-victim-massacre

Cameron Kasky, "Parkland Student: My Generation Won't Stand for This," CNN, February 20, 2018. https://www.cnn.com/2018/02/15/opinions/florida-shooting-no-more-opinion-kasky/index.html

Suzanne Maloney, "Fifteen Years after the 18th of Tir: The Legacy of Student Protests that Shook Iran," Brookings Institute, July 10, 2014. https://www.brookings.edu/blog/markaz/2014/07/10/fifteen-years-after-the-18th-of-tir-the-legacy-of-student-protests-that-shook-iran/

Andrew Marantz, "How Social Media Trolls Turned U.C. Berkeley into a Free-Speech Circus," *The New Yorker*, July 2, 2018. https://www.newyorker.com/magazine/2018/07/02/how-social-media-trolls-turned-uc-berkeley-into-a-free-speech-circus

Malini Ramaiyer, "How Violence Undermined the Berkeley Protest," *New York Times*, February 2, 2018. https://www.nytimes.com/2017/02/02/opinion/how-violence-undermined-the-berkeley-protest.html

Ben Trachtenberg, "The 2015 University of Missouri Protests and Their Lessons for Higher Education Policy and Administration," *Higher Education Today*, June 30, 2018. https://www.higheredtoday.org/2018/07/30/2015-university-missouri-protests-lessons-higher-education/

Stephen J. Wermiel, "A Conversation with Mary Beth Tinker," American Bar Association, March 15, 2012. https://www.americanbar.org/publications/human_rights_magazine_home/human_rights_vol35_2008/human_rights_summer2008/hr_summer08_tinker/

Websites

CampusActivism.org (http://www.campusactivism.org/)
This interactive site features tools for progressive student activists, including those who seek to launch a campaign, share resources, publicize an event, or build networks.

The College Fix (https://www.thecollegefix.com/)
This website provides articles, commentary, and news targeting conservative high school and college students seeking to enter the world of journalism.

Congress of Racial Equality: The Freedom Rides (http://www.core-online.org/History/freedom%20rides.htm)
This site takes readers through the heady and dangerous times forged by mostly student activists in the early 1960s. It explains how they put their lives on the line for the cause of freedom.

Harvard Graduate School of Education: Student Protests (https://www.gse.harvard.edu/news/uk/18/03/ student-protests-questions-and-answers)
The prestigious school offers this question-and-answer site for teachers from which students can learn as well. One can gain knowledge from it about walkouts, free speech, and civic responsibility.

United States Student Association (http://usstudents.org/)
The USSA website for its estimated 1,500,000 members and those interested represents the largest student-led organization in the country. The information found on the site features current student campaigns on various campuses.

Index

Picture Credits

Cover, p. 59 Justin Sullivan/Getty Images; pp. 10, 84 Anadolu Agency/Getty Images; p. 14 Sheila Fitzgerald/Shutterstock.com; p. 20 MediaPunch Inc/Alamy Stock Photo; p. 25 © iStockphoto.com/SteveDebenport; p. 29 Bettmann/Getty Images; p. 35 New York Post Archives/Getty Images; p. 39 Logan Cyrus/AFP/Getty Images; p. 42 Elijah Nouvelage/Getty Images; p. 48 Timothy A. Clary/AFP/Getty Images; p. 53 CQ Roll Call/AP Images; p. 64 stock_photo_world/Shutterstock.com; p. 70 Chip Somodevilla/Getty Images; p. 73 © AP Images; p. 79 Christopher Morris–Corbis/Corbis Historical/Getty Images; p. 92 Scott Olson/Getty Images; p. 100 Michael Candelori/Shutterstock.com